Toni is a powerful coach and her advice and counsel was invaluable in helping me transition into my GM role. Toni is knowledgeable and passionate in what she shares. Working with Toni enabled me to set my focus and confidently step up into opportunities to better lead my team. Toni was a pleasure to work with and I'd work with her again in a heartbeat.

Dina Halkic, General Manager, Fleet Operations, FleetPartners.

Toni has worked across our FleetPartners management teams over the last 18 months delivering a two-day leadership development program, followed by a series of workshops and some executive coaching. The teams were highly engaged with Toni, the feedback has been outstanding, and the question I'm most asked about Toni is Can we have more of her? Toni is highly regarded within our business and we look forward to her continuing to work with us.

Paul Verhoeven, Managing Director,
Group Transformation & Internal Partnerships, Eclipx Group

Toni has an amazing ability to take you to new places you might not have thought were possible. She challenged me, guided me, and then provided me practical models and tools to enable me to focus on the right areas of my work, have better conversations with my staff, and help me achieve my goals.

Liam Palmer-Cannon, Head of Engineering,
Track & Structures, Office of the Chief Engineer, Metro Trains

Working with Toni has been amazing. My leadership has grown so much in the last six months. I'm now more effective, able to think more strategically, and have become intentional in the way I lead. Toni provides practical and relevant tools. I'm inspired by what I've learned from Toni, I feel I'm on the right track again in becoming the leader I want to be. I'd highly recommend Toni as a trainer and coach. I'd love the opportunity to work with her again.

Samantha McNevin, Regional Practice Manager,
HCF Dental Centre Network

INFLUENCE
FROM
THE
INSIDE
OUT

INFLUENCE FROM THE INSIDE OUT

YOUR #1 STRATEGY
FOR GROWING YOUR
LEADERSHIP, VOICE
AND BRAND

TONI COURTNEY

Copyright © Toni Courtney 2018

All models copyright © Toni Courtney 2018

First published in 2018 by Baker Street Press | Melbourne

ISBN 978-0-6482812-3-8

A catalogue record for this book is available from the National Library of Australia

Edited by Joanna Yardley at The Editing House

Typeset by Jane Radman at Jane Radman Designs

YOUR ROAD TO INFLUENCE

STEPPING INTO YOUR BIGGER GAME
AND NEXT LEVEL OF INFLUENCE LIES
WITHIN THREE BUILDING BLOCKS

1

CONNECT
INTO **YOU**

WHO AM I
BEING
FOR ME?

ACKNOWLEDGEMENTS

To my parents, Graham and Margaret, thank you for your unwavering support. Mum, you have been my biggest career champion, especially in this latest career chapter. I don't know what I'd have done without you.

To Sharon Pearson and Joe Pane, thank you for your mentorship through my coach training with the Coaching Institute. I am truly grateful for the difference you have both made in my life.

To the senior executives who generously shared their leadership wisdom and lessons for this book. Your leadership journeys are inspiring, and I want to thank you all for your contribution:

Sally Capp, Lord Mayor of Melbourne
(Former COO, Victorian Chamber of Commerce)

John Coull, Executive Director, Telstra

John Chambers, CEO, Tappl
(Former Executive Director, Telstra)

Kylie Bishop, Group Executive, Medibank

Andrew Dyer, Company Director, National Wind Farm Commissioner for the Australian Federal Government, Professorial Fellow at Monash University

Carlos Schafer, Group Executive, ASG
(Former Executive General Manager,
Open Universities Australia)

Julie Rynski, Customer Executive, NAB
(Former General Manager, Westpac)

Michael Ehrentraut, Executive Director and
COO, Viridian Advisory

Alice Wong, Chair, China Studies Research Centre
Advisory Board, La Trobe University
(Former Head of Asian Leadership, Westpac)

Finally, thank you to all my wonderful clients. I love what I do. Working with you and/or your teams is a privilege for which I am very grateful.

PREFACE

This book is a self-enquiry into how you can become the best version of you and earn the right to have others follow you, so you can make the difference and have the influence and impact you ultimately desire. You'll only get there by discovering what you have in you. The path might be confronting and challenging, but that's the path for your growth and personal development.

I'll be your coach as you work your way through this book. My goal is to challenge, support and champion you for what you believe about you, what you believe is possible for you and what you believe you're ready for. You've got this.

This book is for you if:

1. You feel like you're off track in your career. Your effort, work and commitment haven't paid off like they should have.
2. Other people are getting tapped on the shoulder for new role opportunities and you're missing out.
3. You've believed your results should speak for themselves and now realise they won't.
4. You've been under the radar, and you don't know how to become more visible.
5. You're continually worried about what other people think of you.
6. You have high standards and never seem to meet them.
7. You don't have the leadership voice and presence you want.

8. You know you need to have more influence to get the results you need.
9. Deep inside, you want things to be different.

Whether you want to absorb this book chapter by chapter and go on a journey, or if you'd prefer to the explore chapters in another way, I've written the book to accommodate whichever way you want to read it.

***

When you share your voice, you grow personally and professionally. It's time to realise your value and be heard. Being bold is when your courage is bigger than your fear. It's about saying 'yes' to you, stepping away from the certainty of what you know and having a different voice. It's about tuning into your inner voice that tells you there is more—that you can be more.

Thank you for letting me come on this journey with you. Here's to your success.

INTRODUCTION

**There is no passion to be found playing small
- in settling for a life that is less than the
one you are capable of living.**

— Nelson Mandela

'You've got Polycythaemia Rubra Vera,' I heard my general physician say. 'What's that? Is it serious? 'Well, yes,' he said. I was diagnosed with this chronic bone marrow blood disease while I was pregnant with my daughter.

After I had Kiara, I was at crossroads in my life and career. My partner, at the time, wanted me to find a no-stress, part-time marketing job—a job I could easily handle. But such a change would have felt like giving up on my career while waiting for my disease to take over. Bollocks! I thought. Absolutely not. I would not be a victim to my disease and the ongoing fatigue that would come with it.

Instead I chose to back myself into a new career and, in doing so, I also became a single mum to two young children. After spending 20+ years in senior leadership roles in blue chip corporates, I took what was a massive leap of faith at the time, and I started my own executive coaching and training business. I wanted my life and future to be centred in making a fundamental positive difference to others. That was over five years ago.

It hasn't been beer and skittles; it's been hard, like it is for many women doing it on their own. I'm stronger and more resilient for it though. I would much rather face my life head on than be a bystander. I don't know what my future holds—no one does—but I do know this: I want to look back on my life and appreciate the choices I made through courage, not fear.

It takes courage to grow into who we really are.

—C.C Cummings

I'm continually reminded, by my own corporate journey, and from the privilege of working with my clients, that professional success does not guarantee satisfaction and fulfilment. This comes from within when we decide who we are and live true to our values and principles. Hoping and wishing for empowerment won't get you very far – you have to do the work to empower yourself, and define what success is to you.

Every leader faces adversity. Choosing to back yourself is the most important decision you'll ever make because it involves uncertainty, risk and change. Leading a fulfilling life means doing it for your entire life, but this is easier said than done, especially for women.

LEADERSHIP ISN'T ABOUT TITLE OR POSITION, IT'S ABOUT THE INFLUENCE YOU HAVE.

I don't know anyone who doesn't want to make a positive difference to others, to contribute and add value to something that is bigger than themselves. Our life purpose doesn't need to get any more complicated than that. We have more influence than we think. Our impact on others is greater than we think. Often, we make a profound difference in someone's life without knowing it.

Impacting others positively means influencing them in some way. John Maxwell said that leadership is influence— nothing more, nothing less.[i] We're always influencing; every conversation and interaction allows us to contribute to someone's thinking in some way. Many of my clients perceive that having more influence would improve their leadership effectiveness and want the 'silver bullet' list of influencing strategies and tactics to employ. There is a plethora of books on how to do that. Influence is situational, context dependant and perception based. Having a skill set that enables you to influence is critical, but I believe that influencing—like leadership—is less about what to 'do' and more about how to 'be'. And that's why influence develops from the inside out. Knowing the best tactic to influence someone will be useless if you don't know how to connect with them emotionally and build a trustful relationship.

YOUR LEADERSHIP STARTS WITH THE RELATIONSHIP YOU HAVE WITH YOU; IT DRIVES EVERY RELATIONSHIP YOU HAVE.

Your success isn't determined by your IQ, talent or even potential; it's defined by how well you can lead yourself outside your comfort zone. It's believed that we're typically working to 50% of our potential. I believe we are far more capable than what we give ourselves credit for. We all have a bigger game within us.

Leadership is not for everyone. It's a journey of personal discovery and growth. Growth does not happen to you, it happens within you. Everyone has leadership potential. When you decide who you are and what's important to you, and show up for others from that place, you'll have much more influence. People will want to know who you are. People will want to connect with the real you.

LEADERSHIP IS NOT TELLING OTHERS WHAT TO DO. LEADERSHIP IS INSPIRING OTHERS TO BE THEIR BEST.

Australian research tells us that workplaces that invest in a range of leadership development activities have capable leaders with strong beliefs in their ability to do the job. Both of these factors are linked to better performance and innovation. However, 40% of Australian businesses do not undertake coaching or mentoring programs and 60% do not invest in formal leadership qualifications.[ii]

The pace of work today requires fast decision-making and collaboration. Without influence, your great ideas will go nowhere. As you start off in your career, the results you achieve and deliver through your technical skills matter the most. As you progress into management and leadership, there's a tipping point where your leadership potential is defined by the influence you have. Your success relies on you working with and through others. As you 'become more' in your role, your leadership voice and brand relies on you having influence.

I work with far too many people who can't bridge this gap themselves and who aren't getting the personal and professional development they need within their organisation. They don't have leadership role models to learn from and they don't have a mentor to reach out to for support. Acknowledging this gap was my inspiration for writing this book.

1

CONNECT INTO **YOU**

WHO AM I BEING FOR ME?

CHAPTER 1

YOUR INFLUENCE STARTS WITHIN YOU

IF YOU CHANGE YOUR **THINKING**, YOU'LL CHANGE HOW YOU EXPERIENCE YOUR LIFE.

Who you are today was shaped more by your childhood than you realise. How you think today is a function of your brain's wiring during your formative years when you were developing your self-identity and perceptions of how you fitted in with the world around you.

Leadership doesn't start when you become a leader at work; it starts before that, when your attitude and choices define who

Understanding yourself in the present comes from acknowledging your past. Make peace with your past so it doesn't impact what you want to create in the future.

you are for you, and who you are for others. Leadership is an inside job before it becomes about leading others. The first person you must lead well is you. Like it or not, your thoughts and interpretations of people and events directly influence your beliefs, and ultimately, your leadership actions. Henry Ford said, 'Whether you think you can or cannot, you're right'. In other words, what you think is what you get. It's easy to think of leadership growth in terms learning new skills, becoming more technically competent and gaining experience. While these are important, they'll only get you so far. The most important factor is your mindset.

PEOPLE WITH INFLUENCE CHALLENGE US.

When you think of influential people: who do you think of? Do you think of religious or political figures, scientists and inventors, celebrities or business leaders? Or do you think of significant people closer to home who have shaped your life decisions and career journey so far?

The world's most influential people have changed the fabric of the human existence through their conviction and actions. They teach us. They inspire us. They show us what's important, what we care about, and what's possible. They change how we view the world and how we see ourselves. Take Hitler versus Mother Theresa: no two people could have been further apart in what they stood for and represented; however, the best and worst of human nature and experience is steeped in positive lessons from which we can all learn.

The best type of influence comes from a spirit of humility and generosity because there are lessons for us all in how to be better.

Through life, we're continually influenced by others who shape how we think. We all want to achieve and be successful, yet there's something that we all want more—connection. Whether you love social media or not, Mark Zuckerberg changed our lives forever when he introduced us to Facebook. With over 2 billion monthly users, and nearly 1.5 billion daily users, Facebook is social media's largest and most influential platform—politically and socially. Social media has changed the way we connect, engage, and influence others; it has changed the communication game enabling new and public voices to be heard. Voices from the public who care, who have opinions and who want to be heard just as much as the expert voices who previously ruled.

Through the internet and social media, we can tap into anyone's thinking and grab their attention at any time. The saying that knowledge is power has evolved into attention enables influence. It's the influence someone has that makes them powerful.

YOUR MINDSET DRIVES HOW YOU THINK.

**We don't see the world as it is,
we see it through who we are.**
—Anais Nin

Every sensory experience you have is determined by how you think. Your mindset is your collection of thoughts and beliefs that shape your thought habits. In other words, your mindset drives how you think about anything. The single biggest contributor to your success is your mindset. A high-performance mindset is twice as important to high-performance outcomes as educational background and technical skills.[iii] Your mindset drives your productivity, your confidence, and your courage, how you present yourself, the language you use, and the type of conversations you have. Your mindset impacts everything you do in every part of your life.

There is only one human design; however, no two lives are the same. Carl Yeung said that we can't experience anything outside of us that isn't us. No two people think alike. We all have a unique way of viewing the world—a map, if you like, or a worldview—where we interpret and make sense of what's happening around us by creating meanings or stories as 'our truth'. This map is a filter through which our thinking is created.

The interpretations or meanings we create as the 'truth' can result in us overthinking and overanalysing things. So much so that we simply get in our own way. There is the truth, what actually happened, and then there is what we tell ourselves about it. Our emotional state is fed more by what we tell ourselves about it versus what actually happened. For example, if you don't get that internal promotion, you make it mean you're not valued or rated as highly as you should be. Your ego kicks in and wants to judge and be right; this keeps your inner voice busy and 'on alert'. You feel frustrated and down, and you look for evidence to support your view that shapes your experience of not being valued.

THE MOST IMPORTANT STORIES ARE THE ONES WE TELL OURSELVES. OUR STORIES HELP US STEP INTO OPPORTUNITY OR HINDER US FROM THEM.

The meaning you created, in the example above, was based on your choice of self-doubt. Yet the reality is you might have agreed with the decision not to appoint you, had you known the decision criteria and/or trade-offs made. You can't turn your meanings or stories off, but you can choose the lens through which your story is told. Whether the spin is positive, negative or a bit of both, the choice is always yours.

Your mindset is either your biggest friend or your biggest enemy.

—*Vijaya Vaidyanath, CEO Yarra City Council*

Your mindset shapes how you view yourself and your world, and it shapes how you react and respond in any situation.

How we think is underpinned by our relationship with fear and uncertainty. These relationships and our beliefs about ourselves are formed in our childhood and are influenced by our parents/carers, family members, and teachers (the significant people around us). The consensus is that our script for life is written by the age of four or five, polished by age seven, and lived out from the age of 12.[iv] This wiring, for most of us, dominates how we go on to live our lives.

The relationship we have with ourselves is a result of what we learn and decide about ourselves early on. These decisions are influenced through the lens by which we judge ourselves as good or bad. Then, they form self-beliefs. Our self-beliefs contribute to our internal map, which drives how we think. Our internal map is created from our beliefs, values, past reference points (memories), and various metaprograms.

BEING WHOLE AND COMPLETE MEANS HAVING THE CAPACITY FOR EVERY TRAIT AND EMOTION.

We're born with the capacity for every possible human trait. We have the capacity to hate and love, and to harm and nurture. What we see in others reflects what already exists in within ourselves. For example, when we observe someone displaying kindness, we can only know this because we've already experienced it for ourselves. As children though, we're not taught to appreciate that being whole and complete is having the capacity to experience every possible human trait. Instead, we're conditioned to learn what traits are good and bad and so we can choose those with which we will associate.

Before Christmas, I took my 6-year-old daughter to see Santa. After sitting on his knee and having a chat with him, she assured me that she'd made Santa's 'good' list. Positive traits are positively reinforced, for example, be a good girl and be kind to your brother, while negative traits are punishable or carry the risk of being put down, for example, don't do that to your brother; you're naughty. Children learn quickly what differentiates the good and bad labels by which they're being judged.

It is a common human trait to want to create certainty for ourselves by seeing things as black and white, where we judge something as good or bad, or right or wrong. The payoff is we don't have to see the shades of grey or experience the uncertainty. This habit forms early in life for good reason: children have limited cognitive ability because they lack the life experiences that teach them that shades of grey exist. They only have the cognitive ability for the absolutes and are unable to create the in-between shades of grey the way that adults can.

Children also perceive the world revolves around them. My daughter has a habit of putting herself into any conversation and making it about her. Although this drives me crazy, I know it's perfectly normal.

Children are born wired for love. Without it they cannot thrive. In our quest to receive the love and validation we desire from our parents, we learn to associate into the positive traits, which teach us how we want to see ourselves—as 'good'. Through the process, we disassociate from the negative traits. Consequently, we learn to want to be good and then judge ourselves for being bad. This process plays a massive role in how we begin to develop our earliest self-perceptions. This also creates a tendency and pressure to conform, where we learn to seek external validation instead of internal validation.

DEFINING MOMENTS SHAPE
OUR **SELF-BELIEFS**.

Everyone has typically 5–8 defining moments in their lives. These defining moments can be positive and form the foundation of positive strong self-beliefs, or they can be negative as in the I'm not good enough belief.

Our self-beliefs are created when we give meaning to an event or a defining moment. What we tell ourselves then turns into a belief that shapes who we are and the choices we make. Once we've chosen and decided what that moment means for us, we search for evidence to support the belief with which we associate it. Most of us never question why we still hold the belief or whether it's serving us resourcefully.

Anthony Robbins said the most important opinion a person will ever hold is the one they hold about themselves. Most people never question their beliefs, because they've held onto them for so long. Because our thoughts, behaviours and actions are a direct result of our beliefs, they can work for us (positive self-beliefs) or against us (negative self-beliefs). The good news is that we are free to choose what we believe about ourselves. This means we can create new beliefs, at any time, that will serve us positively in creating the career and life we want to have. In other words, how we defined ourselves as children is not how we have to define ourselves as adults.

OUR BEHAVIOUR IS A CHOICE OF ACTION; IT DOES NOT DEFINE WHO WE ARE.

My mother was a new entrant/prep teacher. She loved her 'little people' and her commitment to her role and opportunity to positively impact her students was inspiring. She understood the importance of the first year of school in laying the foundations of learning and building confidence and self-esteem in children. 'Give me the child until he is seven, and I will give you the man.' —St. Francis Xavier (1506–1552). I remember my mother saying this many times in my life, and I believe it to be true.

My most precious moments with my 8-year-old son are at night when I'm tucking him into bed. Last year he said, 'I'm feeling really sad, Mum. I did a bad thing today'. When I quizzed him about what happened, he replied, 'I was supposed to be doing my work but instead I went to look for a book'. He went on share, 'Lee (his teacher) got cross and growled at me'. His view was that Lee now saw him as being bad. Alex had created his own label. The next day we went to school and chatted with Lee. Lee was able to share that while he thought Alex had made the wrong choice, he still thought Alex was awesome and loved having him in his class. The lesson for Alex was that he was not his behaviour and there was a difference between what he did and who he is.

Unfortunately, unless these sorts of experiences get reshaped for children, they provide a 'moment in time' where they perceive themselves as bad or not good. Children then extrapolate this as there being something wrong with them: I haven't done the right thing, translates to I'm bad, which then translates to a belief of I'm not good enough (or something of similar language).

Your power comes from understanding you and accepting you as you are. You are not all good. You are not all bad. Even though you make choices that you perceive as good or bad, you are not your behaviour. You have strengths and stretches that contribute to who you are. You are always enough.

> Your success comes the day you remember you have everything you need within you. You just need to access it.

Your circumstances don't define you, but your self-beliefs do.

I haven't worked with anyone who, deep down, does not fear not being good enough. And for many, this belief has shaped their whole life: decisions they've made, career choices, relationships — everything.

I once had a colleague who prefaced his good ideas with 'this is probably a silly idea but ....' I learned that as the youngest of three children, his two older brothers, who thought they knew better, squashed his ideas. They told him he was silly and made fun of him, which lead to his disempowering belief that he didn't have anything of value to contribute to anyone.

We're not born with self-beliefs. Every belief we have about ourselves is made up. The I'm not enough belief is universal. Our parents (or significant others), who are our biggest teachers, reflect onto us what they perceive about themselves. This action, as well as the judgements we hear about ourselves from others, is how the I'm not good enough belief is passed on, generation by generation.

If you fear not being good enough, then you're not alone. Everyone else does too.

HOW WE THINK SHAPES WHAT WE BELIEVE ABOUT ANYTHING.

You may not control all of the events that happen to you, but you can decide not to be reduced by them.

—*Maya Angelou*

Your past builds your character; it doesn't define you in the present, but your attitude and decisions do. We are a function of our past. Many heroes come from humble beginnings. Oprah Winfrey, arguably one of the world's most influential woman, experienced a difficult childhood suffering both physical and sexual abuse. As horrific as those childhood events were, she will tell you that what shaped her world, as a child, more than anything was her ability to read at the age of three. Through books, she had the opportunity to delve into another world.

For Oprah, her ability the think beyond her current experience as a child, shaped how she saw her world and the opportunities she believed were possible for herself.

No one has an easy or perfect life. No one holds it together all the time. It's easy to look at someone else and think you know how it is for them and what their life has been like. Judging someone based on their circumstances will always sell them short.

ARE ANY OF THESE SELF-LIMITS FAMILIAR?

I don't know where I'm going in my career.

I've lost enthusiasm for my role.

I don't have the right relationships.

I lack confidence.

I don't have what it takes.

I don't know how to do it.

I'm already working too hard.

I'm too busy.

Now's not the right time.

I don't know what I want.

I've been told this is as far as I'll go.

There are things standing in my way (like my boss, lack of budget, poor systems, the market).

WHAT'S YOUR STORY?

We each have a rich tapestry of life experiences that have shaped who we are and how we think. Acknowledging your past and its influence on you is key to accepting yourself and your internal map of how you think, in the present.

What you think about you and what you believe is possible drives every result you will achieve, underpinned by your relationship with fear, your aptitude for learning and your willingness to take responsibility.

It's easy to judge someone by their behaviour: what they say or do, or don't say or don't do. It's easy to think we know someone, but do we ever? You've heard the golden age saying: don't judge a book by its cover or there is more to someone than meets the eye. How could we possibly truly understand someone without knowing more about what has shaped who they are. Looking past what someone is wearing, and how they are talking is hard but necessary to appreciate who they are.

Everyone has a life story. Being humble isn't about thinking less of yourself. It's realising there's no need to be better than anyone else or try and be like somebody else. Being humble is to appreciate that at some level, we're all the same.

BELIEVING YOU CAN WILL PROPEL YOUR ACTIONS.

Susan Boyle became a household name overnight. There are more than 230 million views of her performance on YouTube. The video clip shows how she stunned her audience (and television viewers) by singing *I dreamed a dream* from *Les Misérables* on Britain's Got Talent. Before she began singing, the audience were mocking her appearance. When Simon Cowell questioned her, she revealed 'I've never been given the chance before' (to sing in front of an audience). Her belief in her chance to shine on stage resulted in her giving the performance of which she dreamed.

ADVERSITY BUILDS CHARACTER.

The ultimate measure of a man is not where he stands in moments of comfort and convenience, but where he stands at times of challenge and controversy.

—*Martin Luther King Jr.*

Your ability to influence is dependent on your credibility and character. Your character will always trump your talent. Your character is reflected by your bruises, your setbacks, and your stuff up's. Your character is your substance: what you were born with and how your circumstances and experiences have shaped you. No one has a free ride in life, and some people seem to face more than their fair share of challenges. The more adversity you have faced, the more character and resilience you have. If you were to draw your life as a line marked by significant life events, what would your line look like? What events and experiences have shaped you the most?

Research suggests that resilience has as much to do with how often people have faced adversity in the past as it does with who they are—their personality, their genes, or what they're facing now. That is, the number of life blows a person has suffered may affect his or her mental toughness more than any other factor.

GREAT LEADERS HAVE DEPTH.

Great leaders have learnt through diverse experience—positive and negative—to be able to appreciate context and complexity.

What you bring to your job and that of which you are capable is far more than what you've learnt on the job. It's a result of your life story that has shaped who you are and how you think.

Everyone is good at something. Everyone has strengths to tap into. It's just most people don't know what they're good at because they spend so much time perceiving their 'not good enough' at something. It's thought that mastery takes 10,000 hours of practice. I believe we all have 10,000 hours' worth of experience in something that we know. We simply don't realise it in this context. A client reminded me recently that, during our first conversation, I mentioned I was good at what I did. She reflected afterward on what I'd said. She admired my confidence and certainty, and she realised that she'd never told anyone, after 10 years' experience in her field, that she considered herself to be good at what she did.

I believe that you know more than you think, you are more capable than you think, and you are more resilient than you think. I'm teaching my children that 'they can'. I've eliminated the response of 'I can't' when they attempt to do something they are afraid they can't do. Instead, we focus on having a go, having another go, and getting better with practice and persistence. I acknowledge the effort they have made along the way, as well as the result achieved—whatever that is.

I was inspired hearing Alisa Camplin (who won Australia's first ever medal in a Winter Olympic Games for aerial skiing in 2002) speak about her journey to win gold. Before being invited into the Olympic team, she'd never skied before. She suffered bitterness from those who thought her motivation for joining the sport was wrong. Many aerial skiers mocked her lack of skills. 'It took seven years of my eight-year campaign before people began to believe that I might actually be able to win an Olympic Gold medal,' she said. Through everything she did to prepare herself for gold, there was one thing she never did—she never gave up believing in the possibility that she could win.

Your attitude about what's on your plate, your belief about what's possible, and what you believe you can do, will be the making of you as a person and as a leader.

WE'RE BORN TO EXPERIENCE LOVE; WE LEARN TO EXPERIENCE FEAR.

I believe we are wired for love and (psychological) safety. Babies are alert as soon as they learn they exist as a separate entity detached from their mother. This instinctual mechanism works for us and against us through our need for certainty that allows us to feel safe.

The environment of your childhood shaped your relationship with learning, fear and possibility. Did you grow up in an environment that supported your curiosity to be able to give things a go without the fear of being good or bad or getting it right or wrong? Did your parents or carers notice what you'd done and encouraged your progress or effort, or did they notice if something was wrong and told you how to make it right? I was working with a client recently who shared a deeply engrained lesson from his parents. They continually told him, as a child, to show people how good he was by what he did and by getting it right. Needless to say, the need to 'get it right' to prove he was good enough was lived out through his fear of making a mistake and getting it wrong. This construct for how he lived his life impacted every area of it—including his leadership. Now, as a senior leader, he appreciates the opportunity to 'get out of his own way' through redefining his leadership identity as the first step. Without this development, his career will not progress.

LEARNING AND LEADERSHIP GO HAND IN HAND.

We learn through doing; this makes us curious and resilient. My son's process of learning how to walk fascinated me. He fell and got back up repeatedly, sometimes hurting himself in the process. Toddlers don't question the need to get back up after they fall down. They don't know the concept of giving up. They do what it takes to learn to walk.

Research shows that children who are given opportunities to take risks and explore helps them develop a healthy relationship with learning.[v] Childhood experiences shape how we learn to experience fear, which shapes our lens for learning. We know that fear and learning are mutually exclusive. Children only learn in an environment that is safe and supportive.

YOUR LENS FOR LEARNING IS A CRITICAL COMPONENT OF YOUR LEADERSHIP DEVELOPMENT.

Your appetite, aptitude and attitude for learning, receiving feedback and personal growth are shaped by your formative years and result in your current assumptions about learning.

**If I'm learning, I'm asking questions.
I don't care about the organisational hierarchy.
I learn from people more senior, junior and peer level
– I value the contribution of others. This attitude has
opened my mind up to incredible possibility.
Learning is not linear, it's not narrow.**

—Kylie Bishop

My son has a love for books; he has at least a dozen scattered on one side of his bed. From an early age, he's gone to bed with books. However, he has found learning to read a challenge and his progress has been slower than expected. At the beginning of the year, I spoke with his teacher and commented that my goal for Alex for the school year was for him to meet the minimum benchmark to enable him to get into Grade 3 the following year. His teacher challenged me. He explained that a more empowering goal for Alex was to encourage his love and thirst for reading. I understood this feedback in the context of his attitude being the basis for his lens for learning. I've had to appreciate that my persistence in getting him to know basic words has contributed to an environment where his attitude toward reading at home has been less than ideal over the past year. My wanting him to 'get the words right' versus enjoying the process of reading, having a go, and not worrying about accuracy wasn't helping him.

First things first: attitude before accuracy is what I now remind myself of, knowing how important it is for him to enjoy reading, and being able to find a balance along the track where is he able to read with accuracy too. If I don't get this balance right, his belief that 'he's getting it right or wrong' will shape his experiences in life to a much greater degree than they should.

ARE YOU A LEADER WHO LISTENS?

Consider this distinction in a recent *Forbes* article: Successful leaders listen as a way to see more clearly their own part in the problem at hand, and to understand how to stretch beyond their limitations and grow. Poor leaders listen only as a way to defend and justify who they have become. [vi]

Last year at the beginning of a work training session where I was the trainer, a participant put up his hand and asked me how old I was? Before I had the chance to quiz him on his purpose for asking, he stated his assumption that he was older than I was, inferring that with age comes wisdom. He then told me, 'I'll listen to you, but I don't have to agree with what you say'. Someone who listens to judge will either accept or reject the information provided. What do you think their capacity for learning is versus someone who is prepared to try something on, on the basis of it's me.

In any situation—work, life, relationships—choose to focus on the opportunity to learn, grow and become the next better version of you.

THE BEST LEARNING FRAME IS IT'S ME.

Where you are willing to think and willing to learn? When you are a functional learner anything is possible.

Whenever I'm recruiting someone into my team I not only evaluate what they will contribute to the team, I also evaluate their potential to contribute to me, the leader. What are you going to teach me? How can you stretch me and help me learn? This is a muscle for learning that supports my belief that everything I do is about learning.

—John Coull

I met someone last year who proactively changes roles every two years. When I quizzed him on his purpose for this, he shared that his aim was to fast-track his learning. He believes this is a necessary step in order to learn at the speed he enjoys and wants. He views his career as a learning experience; this is his priority. He appreciates the inherent risk in his strategy given that he needs to start from scratch so frequently and prove himself.

HOW EASY IS IT FOR YOU TO BE SELF-EXPRESSED?

The degree to which you were self-expressed as a child impacts your ability to have a voice and be self-expressed as an adult. Your ability to self-express and have a voice is the starting point of having influence.

As a consequence of a lack of boundaries for self-expression in my childhood, (when I was in trouble, I was punished without being allowed a voice—a common occurrence in my era I think), I've found it hard to express myself as an adult and have a voice in situations where there is perceived conflict involving figures of perceived authority. I'm pretty good at backing myself; however, when it comes to confronting people whom I perceive to be authority figures, or more senior or more influential, this pattern shows up for me.

When my pattern of shutting down surfaces it impacts my ability to have a voice. A few months ago, I was introduced to a woman who was in a position to offer me an opportunity:

she was looking for help, and I was looking for work. She was hosting a breakfast and I was invited. At the event, she presented some great leadership content about how injecting others with short term boosts of motivation doesn't work. A few weeks later, she called me. I was expecting an offer of work. Instead, she wanted to talk about a blog I'd written that week. She believed I had plagiarised her content from the breakfast event. She was angry and offended, and she told me, directly, how she felt. Instead of sticking up for myself and sharing how the content was referenced by other content I'd previously written, I fell into my old pattern of shutting down, shutting up and having no voice. In fact, while she was giving me her feedback, I didn't question her about her assumptions about where the content of my blog had come from.

Understanding yourself in the present comes from understanding your experiences in the past that have shape how you think.

OUR POTENTIAL FOR LEADERSHIP IS SHAPED THROUGH OUR LIVES.

There are many ways to learn about leadership and increase your capacity for it. Think about the teams you have participated in like sports, scouts, school councils etc. Some of our best learning happens outside of work, without formal hierarchy of authority (in the traditional sense). For example, a community group of volunteers, where people give their time to be of service, provides an opportunity to learn how to work with others, and engage and influence others because people don't **have** to work with you—people work with you because they **want** to. Years ago, I participated in an 'outside of work' leadership group. I had the most (traditional) leadership experience of anyone. I learned that what I said didn't matter. What mattered the most was how I led with humility and respect, and how I gave value that allowed others to contribute.

WHO WE ARE AND WHO WE'RE BECOMING IS BASED ON HOW WE PERCEIVE OUR PAST, PRESENT AND FUTURE.

How you think shapes your relationship with you, and your relationship with fear, uncertainty and risk. Having a functional map for how you think is the key to beginning to build your influence.

How do your thoughts and conclusions play out in your life? What is the behaviour attached to those thoughts? Does that behaviour match up with who you want to be?

By understanding how you think and what's driving your behaviour, you can begin to create the version of yourself you want to become in the future, as well as the future you want to have. Let's begin this conversation by moving into Chapter 2.

CHAPTER 2

ARE
YOU
READY
TO
LEAN IN?

WE ARE ALWAYS INFLUENCING.

Everyone has influence. Regardless of who you are, your title, and whether you manage or lead others, you have influence with the people around you. We are social and emotional beings. The very nature of communication is to impart information in order to shape someone else's thinking; therefore, we're always influencing. People are continually reacting to what you say or do even if you don't like or appreciate the reaction.

Even though you may not have a position of influence, you are in position to influence. That makes you a leader.

—John Maxwell

There may be times when you don't feel particularly influential, or times when you feel you're just one part of a greater whole. These are the times when you're tempted to believe your voice doesn't matter, your insights don't count, and your ideas aren't welcomed.

Leadership is hard. No one knows your intentions or how hard you're trying. Even if you believe you're demonstrating a competency, if no one else is experiencing it, then to others, you don't have it. Your ability to engage and influence others to achieve results is what counts. Leadership is about what you're prepared to give to positively impact someone else.

YOUR ATTITUDE AND PERCEPTIONS
ARE ALWAYS YOUR CHOICE.

Ask yourself the following three fundamental leadership questions to ascertain where you and your leadership are:

1. What am I taking responsibility for?
2. Where is my focus?
3. Where do I live emotionally?

ARE YOUR INNER REACTIONS WORKING FOR OR AGAINST YOU?

The truth of where we live emotionally is determined by our inner reactions to what happens in our life. Our inner reactions are based on our beliefs. In other words, we become what we react to.

Our real thoughts and feelings are messy, raw. They're far less functional than we'd ever reveal to others, and far from the polished 'looking good' image (of ourselves) we show to others. However, our inner thoughts and feelings create our reality and experiences.

For most of us, our inner dialogue has become so habitual that we don't even notice it. We don't notice the influence it has on how we're living our life, and we falsely conclude that life is 'just the way it is'. When in reality, it's just how we've created it over and over again by using the same dialogue.

How much of your time do you spend on autopilot, going through the motions, feeling like work is just a list of tasks or things to get done? Or waiting for Friday to arrive? Alternatively, what part of your work is worth doing? What is the work that matters to you the most?

All great businesses and teams have leaders worth following, cultures worth belonging to and work worth doing.

— Matt Church

When we do work worth doing, we're doing work we care about. We feel motivated, engaged and inspired. Lasting motivation comes from within, not from an exciting new project or your boss telling you that you can do it. Shots of motivation are short lived.

If we break down the work we care about, we have four ingredients:

1. **Challenge**: enables us to think differently.
2. **Responsibility**: grow our skills, relationships and contribute to others.
3. **Autonomy**: we're in control of our own choices as we move through our work.
4. **Sense of progress:** where there is a connection between our effort and the outcome.

We care about this sort of work because we make a positive difference to others, our organisation, and ourselves.

SUCCESS IS NEVER ACHIEVED ALONE;
IT'S ALWAYS THROUGH OTHERS.

We're creatures of habit. We do things the same old way because it's comfortable, and it's what we know. We don't have to question it. Our comfort zone is filled with safety, predictability and certainty. We all need a comfort zone. Can you imagine being on high alert day after day? It would be stressful and exhausting. No one has that amount of adrenalin.

What is your status quo, and where are your comfort zones?

- Are you getting the results you want?
- Are you where you thought you'd be or do you feel like you're off track?
- Are you as confident as you'd like to be?
- Do you have the tough conversations you need to?
- Are you giving the critical performance feedback you want to?
- Do you express your ideas and opinions freely?
- Do you put yourself forward for the opportunities you want to pursue?

Your growth and development sit outside your comfort zone. The degree to which you're prepared to grow is the degree to which you're prepared to feel uncomfortable. The secret here, of course, is to find the balance that gives you stability to grow and develop outside your comfort zone.

Maybe it didn't go how you wanted it to. Maybe it ended badly. Maybe you wished it was different. What if you focused on what you learnt? Or how you grew? Or that you actually tried? You went into it for a reason. Own the decision and the outcome. They were yours to make—good or bad. If you take the credit for success, then you have to be prepared to take responsibility for the result when you don't win.

—Sharon Pearson

IS SOMEONE HOLDING YOU BACK?
IS IT YOU?

Because we are risk adverse by nature, 'thinking about it' seems more natural than 'having a go' and risking making mistakes. We think, ponder, study and gain no progress. It's only when we ignore our instinct to 'play it safe' that we free ourselves to be, have and give all of who we are.

Our greatest victories are won not over circumstances or other people but over ourselves.

—*Doug Grady*

I work with many clients who want things to be different. They feel stuck. Do you feel like that? Is there something you're holding off from saying or doing? For example, not giving the feedback, not saying what you think, not putting your hand up or not taking the risk? So many people wait for the right time, the right words, the right way or the right approach. But holding off costs them time, productivity, money, momentum or something else.

It's easy to judge or criticise others around us. It's far less easy to look at ourselves accurately and to have no ego in the feedback we give ourselves. As Nassim Nicholas Talab writes in his book *Antifragile*, 'To be sophisticated, you need to accept that you are not so'.

Wishing, hoping and waiting for things to change disempowers you. You give up the opportunity to make a difference, be the example, or take the lead. The situation might not be entirely in your control; however, you can control you. How you react and respond reflects the leadership standards you adhere to for yourself.

HOW MANY OF YOUR PROBLEMS ARE WORTH WORRYING ABOUT? IT ALL STARTS WITH HOW YOU THINK.

Problems are defined by the thinking that created them. If you change how you think about a problem, the problem will change. A problem for someone will be an opportunity for someone else. Problems don't exist in physicality.

I remember participating in a leadership group with no hierarchy—we were on an equal basis. We were given a list that outlined the standards by which we were expected to contribute; most people were not meeting the standards, and it wasn't fair on others who were. They were the standards we all created and signed up for. I was waiting for someone to come in and sort the situation out. We couldn't go on like that. It came as an 'aha' moment for me to realise that the person I was waiting for was me. I led the conversation about standards we had all previously agreed on, giving everyone an opportunity to meet them, and when they weren't met, people knew they were going to be removed from the team. We went from a team of ten to four in a few weeks. I didn't enjoy it, and it was a great lesson in holding myself and others accountable. It also hit home for me how leadership isn't about being liked or being popular, it's about being effective.

I focus on what I want to do. I do the things that no one else wants to do. I do the things people say I can't do. I do the things I say I can't do either. I keep pushing on, through setbacks, because I'm clear about what I want to achieve and contribute to others.

—Alice Wong

INFLUENCE BEGINS WITH WHAT YOU'RE PREPARED TO TAKE RESPONSIBILITY FOR.

Think of the narrow-minded people with whom you've worked. They don't listen to the opinions of others, they get fixated on a particular point of view or outcome and won't be persuaded otherwise. Underpinning this pattern of behaviour is the need to be right and to justify why it's so; they play the blame game. I often hear the culture being blamed, or the leadership team—something external to them. As a result, they are challenging to work with. Their mindset is narrow and fixed. They're more focused on themselves and 'getting' from others what they perceive they want and need. They hide their real concerns.

Blaming can also be addictive, because it makes us feel powerful and keeps us from having to examine our own role in a situation. Where there is blame though, there is no learning.

BLAMING SOMEONE ELSE NEVER SOLVES YOUR PROBLEM.

Research suggests that the number one indicator of your potential and success is evident in your pattern of 'external or internal'. For example, when you have a problem, do you think about it in terms of the responsibility or the solution? Is it something that will come from within you (internal) or are you waiting for your environment and others around you to change (external)? Anyone who externalises their results and non-results, gives themselves little power to change.

Stanford University psychologist Carol Dweck undertook decades of research on achievement and success and she distinguished two key mindsets: a growth versus fixed mindset. Other mindset models you might be familiar with use the phrase above the line thinking versus below the line thinking.

Someone with a growth or adaptive mindset sees challenge as opportunity. They take responsibility for their results. They bring an attitude to learn and grow and they appreciate that their effort and persistence will pay off, so they choose to be positive about themselves and their future. They believe they can improve. And they know mistakes will happen.

Carol Dweck's inquiry into beliefs is summarised in *Mindset: The New Psychology of Success*. The book explores how our conscious and unconscious thoughts affect us and how something as simple as wording can have a powerful impact on our ability to improve.

Whatever success you want, your mindset needs to reflect the beliefs that things can change, that you can improve, and that you can lead the change. What you tell yourself matters.

HOW DO YOU RELATE TO THESE POSITIVE SELF-BELIEFS?

I'm good to great.

I'm curious.

I can think on my feet.

I'm passionate about what I care about.

I can listen deeply.

I can say what needs to be said with confidence.

I have the courage I need.

I'm responsible.

There is always progress to make.

THE ONLY PERSON WHO CAN STEP INTO YOUR POTENTIAL IS YOU.

We're always growing and developing in some way, shape or form. Think of the version of you, you were five or ten years ago. The version of you today has been shaped by every experience you've had in those five to ten years.

We each have two versions of ourselves. There is the version that is our surface self, where we go through our day never questioning our experiences and 'getting by'. I think we can all relate to this version of ourselves, where 'it is what it is' and things 'are the way they are'. In contrast, is our ideal self. This is the version of ourselves that wants to break free, be fulfilled and have meaningful experiences, where life is different, better. What sits between our surface self and our ideal self is our self-esteem: our value as a result of the relationship we have with ourselves and the degree to which we believe we're worthy.

Carol Dweck's work shows the power of our most basic beliefs. Whether conscious or subconscious, they strongly 'affect what we want and whether we succeed in getting it'. Much of what we think we understand of our personality comes from our mindset. This both propels us and prevents us from fulfilling our potential.

Again, I want to ask you, where are you at? Do you want to change your status quo? In the context of your leadership, who are you as a leader and who do you want to become as a leader? For things to be different, you need to look beyond your current state, comfort zone, assumptions and beliefs for how things are, and how you are.

What got you here may not get you there.

—*Dr Marshall Goldsmith*

WHAT YOU FOCUS ON IS WHAT YOU GET.

If you focus on how hard something is, and how impossible it seems, or how you never think you're going to get there, that's the thing you're going to experience more of. You'll essentially create the experience of your reality as the thing you don't want.

If you focus on fear, you'll experience more fear. For example, what if they actually offer me this job, and I stuff it up? Should I apply for it or not?

If you fear change, you'll create more fear. For example, what if this new system doesn't work and we get the blame?

Are your decisions driven from your thoughts or feelings? Don't let your feelings override your decisions. Own your feelings; you don't have to try and feel positive if you don't want to. Accept your feelings as they are and make the decision to act in a way that's positive for you anyway. It's worth asking yourself, how would I like to feel? What needs to happen for me to feel like that? We choose our feelings, and we can choose to change how we're feeling instantly. Our feelings are not a fixed state.

In his TEDxBloomington Talk, *The Happy Secret to Better Work*, Shawn Achor says, 'if you can raise somebody's level of positivity in the present, then their brain experiences what we now call a happiness advantage, which is your brain at positive performs significantly better than at negative, neutral or stressed. Your intelligence rises, your creativity rises, your energy levels rise. In fact, we've found that every single business outcome improves. Your brain at positive is 31 % more productive than your brain at negative, neutral or stressed'.

YOU DON'T HAVE TO BE IN A DESIGNATED LEADERSHIP ROLE TO LEAD.

Learning about leadership happens well before you are responsible for others. The best way to learn leadership is to manage projects where you gain hands-on experience and learn on the job. Chris, a client of mine, was a Change Manager for a large health insurance company. He was assigned a significant project to implement a new core system that would improve processes within the front line. However, some of the departments and leaders didn't see the new system was warranted, and they didn't support the change he was brought in to facilitate. Chris quickly realised the question he had to answer for himself was how can I do my job of making change when the people who actually run the department don't want to change? The answer he arrived at was influence.

Learning leadership isn't about having a team. It's about collaborating through the organisation, being able to influence, and win the hearts and minds of others that don't work for you in a way that they want to help. It's about selling the vision, motivating others to come and work with you and engaging them along the way.

—Andrew Dyer.

FOR THINGS TO WORK OUT,
YOU NEED TO PUT THE WORK IN.

Most of us don't know what we want in our career or life. As a result, we often have poor goals and wonder why things aren't working out the way we want. We also have a habit of comparing ourselves to others in a way that either judges them or ourselves negatively. Not only that, we also look at what someone has done to achieve their success and wrongly assume that if we replicate their actions, we'll achieve the same or similar result. All of this thinking is flawed.

Success is a strategy played through the game you play. Success leaves clues. Breaking down someone's success to reveal the true picture for how they've achieved what they have, involves studying their thinking and actions (in Chapter 8, there is a breakdown for how to do this).

YOUR SUCCESS DIMENSIONS	DESCRIPTION	EXAMPLES
Who you are	Your **mindset** (how you think)	Your character (attitudes, beliefs, values)
What you can give	Your **competencies** (what you can do)	Your influencing competencies: • leadership • problem solving • managing change • negotiating • coaching • communication
What you're prepared to do	Your **strategies** (what you plan)	Your goals (intentions)
	Your **actions** (what you do)	Your opportunities to accomplish, achieve, and make a difference (or however you define what success is for you)

TABLE 1: THE DIMENSIONS OF SUCCESS

Each of the success dimensions in the table above need to be in place for you to build your leadership voice and have the positive influence and impact you desire. Taking personal responsibility ties these dimensions together. Your results will always be a reflection of your habits: how you think, how you plan, how you consistently take action. Your greatest assets are your mind and time. How you use them will make or break what you can achieve.

DO YOU SEE YOURSELF AS A LEADER?

How do you relate to yourself as a leader? Is leadership something you aspire to or something you are pursuing now? How you see yourself is important. If you don't see yourself as a leader, then why should other people?

Leadership is a commitment to do what it takes to become one with humility, compassion and patience. There aren't any shortcuts or silver bullets. This is why leadership is so hard and why so few people become leaders who can influence, impact and inspire.

**Leadership is having skin in the game
– a lot of people don't want leadership because
it comes with lots of responsibility.
Being a leader is being prepared to fail.
If you don't put yourself in a leadership position,
you will only fail with others, but if you are the one
running with the ball, at the end of the day
you are holding the ball. It's about taking
responsibility and taking risks.**

—Carlos Schafer

THE REALITY IS THAT LEADERSHIP IS NOT FOR EVERYONE (AND THAT'S OKAY).

There tends to be an expectation, particularly in corporate environments, that people want to climb the career ladder and as a consequence, step into leadership. I feel strongly that people, especially women shouldn't feel the need to assume a leadership title to gauge their success. Aligning your life and career choices to what you care about the most is deeply personal.

Paula Kerger, CEO of American firm PBS, offers this advice: 'find your inner voice—the voice that tells you what your passion is and what you want in life—and listen to it'. [vii]

You don't need a big life plan or career plan. You don't need to have everything figured out. Most people don't, but you might not be as off track as you think you are.

ARE YOU READY TO LEAN IN?

Have you ever noticed how some people pursue their dreams while others struggle to get out of their comfort zone, even though they say they want things to be different? There's a difference between intention and results. It's why the diet industry will always make money. For some, there are millions of calories between wanting to lose weight and watching the kilo's drop off.

To create change, we need to feel enough discomfort and we do that by assessing, for example, the cost if things don't change. Anthony Robbins, in his book, *Awaken the Giant Within*, talks about a force that is controlling your every action: pain and pleasure, everything you do is either out of your need to avoid pain or your desire to gain pleasure.

Anthony Robbins talks about procrastination as an example: when you put something off for so long and then suddenly, the deadline looms and you feel pressure to get it done. What happened? You simply changed what you linked pain and pleasure to. The consequences of not making the deadline were far higher than the decision to continue to procrastinate.

NO ONE LIKES CHANGE.

We prefer predictability and comfort. You have to really want what it is you're moving toward. The only way to move from where you are to where you want to be is to take responsibility for getting there. You need to put yourself in a painful place of responsibility. You are the only person who can take responsibility for your growth and development. You can't change anyone else but yourself. You have to be the one to make the next move. Don't wait until the time is right. Don't wait until you're less busy. You won't be. You don't need anyone's permission to take a step forward into the next stage of your leadership or professional development. You just need to prioritise and say yes to you.

Do you need more experience on the job to learn how to do it better, and improve your relationships and influence along the way? Or do you need to have the courage to put your hand up for the opportunities that are going to scare you but will help you the most?

The first step is to realise, appreciate and accept where you are without judgement. I was working with Sally. She'd been in her role for four years, and she'd worked hard to improve her results and build a reputation for being a well-regarded, reliable, solid performer. But all Sally could see were her colleagues being promoted around her. She believed that she'd fallen behind. As we began to work together, Sally realised there were some areas she needed to develop in before she was going to get a tap on the shoulder for a promotion. Her current role offered her the growth she needed. Sally changed her perspective from one where she thought she'd been left behind, to one where she was empowered to develop from her current status.

It's easy to think the next job, relationship, or house will be better and that once we've 'gotten' what we want, we'll be satisfied. It's a trap. We assume the grass is going to get greener but often this is false hope that never changes, because we're always looking forward to a better future state, rather than accepting and valuing what we have right now. Truth is, if you don't love your current state, you can't love a future state. For example, body image is so low in Australia that a Special K #OwnIt Body Confidence survey has revealed that seven out of ten women have an I hate my body moment every single week. [viii]

The only way to learn to love your body is to decide to love you now. In other words, you can't 'be' satisfied and love your ideal future self, if you're not satisfied and don't love yourself now. If you only ever chase the future ideal, you'll never be satisfied with the now. When you hit that future state, it won't be enough.

Your awareness of what will hold you back from your bigger game is your starting point. Our biggest challenge is often getting over our own fears, anxieties and ourselves. No one is perfect. To play a bigger game, we need to stop defending why we can't or won't play bigger now. It's a choice we control regardless of the challenges we face and things we can't control that might impact our game.

WHAT IS THE NEXT BEST VERSION OF YOU, WHO DO YOU WANT TO BECOME?

Becoming a true leader is bringing your best and whole self to work. You can only experience true fulfilment at work when you're prepared to bring all of you into what you do. Connecting into you means being connected into who you are for you, and how you want to show up for others.

PLAYING BIGGER STARTS WITH A DIFFERENT MINDSET.

People who achieve aren't any smarter or more talented than you. They discern what is important, take responsibility and are prepared to do the work. Isn't it better to play big, to step into the possibility of what might be, as opposed to the smaller game of certainty? What if the long shot played out?

Play big because the game is a different mindset. Ultimately, your ability to embrace uncertainty and step outside your comfort zone will drive your growth.

Success is not actually built by moving from hit to hit to hit. It's the batting average that counts.

—*Satya Nadella, Microsoft CEO*

How prepared are you to step out of your comfort zone by being bold and creating positive change that you lead, rather than a process you manage or execute? Are you waiting for opportunity to present itself or are your leadership opportunities waiting for you?

IT'S YOUR JOB TO BRING YOUR BEST SELF TO WORK. NO ONE ELSE CAN.

Developing accountability skills is challenging; it takes courage and the willingness to learn new ways of thinking and acting. Stop waiting to become empowered. Waiting for things to change in your favour, and being too busy, is just hiding. You can empower yourself right now by accepting who you are, where you're at, and deciding who you want to become.

The degree to which leadership influence evolves is a function of how well you know and understand yourself and what you're prepared to take responsibility for. It's that simple. Are you ready to lean in to your bigger game?

CHAPTER 3

LEADERSHIP: A JOURNEY OF SELF-AWARENESS AND PERSONAL GROWTH

A LEADER WITHOUT **SELF-AWARENESS** IS ON THEIR OWN.

It takes a fair amount of natural ability to reach senior leadership levels. While leadership is learned, it's not an even playing field. What separates effective leaders from those who never make leadership ranks cannot be learned. For example, you can't teach someone to value personal responsibility, to care for others, or to have a thirst for learning. These characteristics are part of someone's core character and personality.

BRINGING YOUR BEST SELF TO WORK MEANS UNDERSTANDING YOU AND BEING YOU.

When you've been at your best in the past, what's been happening for you to experience that? What enables you to thrive and be your best self? I believe we all want to experience the same three things at work:

1. Doing what we love (with people we enjoy being around).
2. Feeling happy (knowing that we are valued and that we have a sense of belonging).
3. Being fulfilled (believing our contribution is helping towards a greater good).

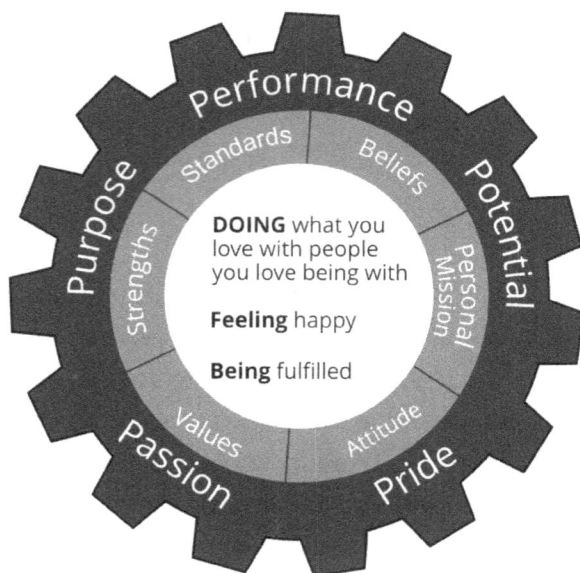

FIGURE 1: BRING YOUR BEST SELF TO WORK MODEL

The following elements bring your best self to life: passion, purpose, performance, potential, pride, determination, persistence, and courage. Everyone has these qualities but some people simply turn them up when they are needed, especially in the face of fear.

You are not a human 'doing'. We are a human 'being'. When you bring your best self to work you can:

- be clear and certain about what you want to achieve and why it's important
- bring the passion that can ignite the same in others
- realise your potential sooner
- thrive and feel a deep sense of self-pride and self-respect.

THE MOST IMPORTANT QUALITY OF LEADERSHIP IS SELF-AWARENESS.

Many leaders go through times when they're working hard and doing all the right things, but their traction and effectiveness isn't hitting the mark. They're not sure what's getting in the way and they realise that trying harder at the same thing isn't getting better results. As we explored in Chapter 2, it's easier to blame others than it is to look within ourselves. More often than not, however, the crux of the problem is a leader's lack of self-awareness to acknowledge and understand the problem lies within them. The leader is simply not seeing what everyone else is seeing.

We all have blind spots, areas of which we are unaware. They impact the way we listen, communicate, and our overall effectiveness in working with others. It's far easier to judge someone else for their blind spots or development needs, than it is to spot them within ourselves. Often there are subtleties and 'fine lines' in our behaviour and tone that create a (small or large) disconnect between our intention and impact. Usually we don't see the gap until there are negative consequences.

THE MORE WE LEARN ABOUT OURSELVES, THE BETTER WE CAN BE FOR OTHERS.

Research has shown that self-awareness is a leadership quality that trumps any other. Self-awareness is the key to emotional intelligence, personal growth, confidence (covered in Chapter 4) and self-mastery. Being self-aware means knowing and understanding you: your strengths, vulnerabilities, blind spots, and motivations for example.

Ross was a newly appointed Head of Sales and found his first six months challenging as he transitioned into his role. While he quickly became involved in many projects, he never seemed to adapt to the culture. With multiple demands on his time and how he experienced being 'busy', others perceived him as blunt to the point of being rude and sometimes lacking empathy. Consequently, he didn't develop trust within his team and seemed to be disconnected from them. To make things worse, it seemed to his team members that he didn't know how to be a senior leader because his peers often pushed him around; they felt he was a yes leader who wasn't prepared to back the team.

Ross's first team engagement scores weren't great. Someone from HR had a catch up with the team to seek feedback. As a result, Ross realised that his team wanted to be heard and understood. Each team member wanted to know that their contributions and opinions mattered. He saw that he needed to step up and learn to connect genuinely with others to build effective relationships.

Ross knew that he had to start leading by example. For the first time in years he evaluated his own leadership stretches and decided to commit to a new set of expectations for himself based on how he wanted to show up for others. As a result, he turned things around and earned the right to lead his team.

Leadership is a journey of personal development marked by stages of self-awareness—no one can teach you how to become better. The only person who can lead you to make positive change is you. Leadership doesn't happen, you make 'it' happen through what you're prepared to do and learn along the way. There is no point of arrival, for anyone.

Core to the leadership journey is moving from self-focus to others-focus. What enables this move of progress from self to others is self-awareness.

YOU CAN'T INFLUENCE OTHERS IF YOU'RE MAKING IT ALL ABOUT YOU.

Everyone starts their career being self-focused. It makes sense. We're learning everything for the first time: new skills, navigating relationships, working with a boss, and being part of a new cultural environment. Then, we improve. We get technically better and more competent. Our results improve, and we gain confidence. We want to do more. We want more. We're ready for new challenges. Through the process, our focus is on ourselves, our needs, and having things go our way. We meet our own needs first. We achieve results and achieve individual success, even as part of a team. Quickly though, achieving results becomes about working with and through others.

Influence is not about getting.
It's about giving. Be realistic about who we are.
I've seen too many people get big titles
and big cars and all the things that come with
the big jobs, and I've seen that go to people's heads
like a drug and forgetting who they are.
Leadership for me is the role of servant.
I serve the people who serve our customers.

—John Coull

If you google the definition of leadership, you will return over thirteen million results. While there is no single agreed definition, no one can argue that leadership, in the context of leading a team, is about focusing on others. A common phrase is servant leadership, coined by Robert K. Greenleaf 1970. In essence, servant leadership is about putting others first and serving the needs of others before your own. This does not mean your needs don't count. Of course they do. It simply means the role of the leader is about meeting the needs of others before meeting your own, which is about creating certainty for others. The contrast frame is the old school 'command and control' type of leadership where it was all about the leader, their sense of power and control, and their certainty. Their focus was on themselves before others. Many leaders are still operating in this space or versions of it to a more or lesser degree.

WE ALL HAVE THE SAME NEEDS.

In the work place, people are looking for certainty from their reporting leader so they feel psychologically safe:

- People want to know they belong.
- People want to know they are valued.
- People want to know their contribution is toward a greater good.

Great leaders give others certainty, especially when times are tough and when things go wrong. They share their perspective in a way that enables people to be okay, feel okay, and know everything is okay.

In the spirit of trust, everything becomes possible.

In *The Daily Stoic*, by Ryan Holiday and Stephen Hanselman, one day's entry is about the idea that calm is contagious. Here are the author's words from the book:

'There is a maxim that Navy SEALs pass from officer to officer, person to person. In the midst of chaos, even in the fog of war, their battle-tested advice is this: "Calm is contagious". Especially when that calm is coming from the man or woman in charge. If the men begin to lose their wits, if the group is unsure of what to do next, it's the leader's job to do one thing: instill calm—not by force but by example.'

People have their needs met when their leader is calm, patient, judgement free and able to use sound judgement in ways that create psychological safety for them. These four core leadership benchmarks came from Sharon Pearson, CEO of The Coaching Institute, and I've shared them with many of my clients as the foundation from which to lead. These benchmarks are not mutually exclusive. When we're emotionally charged our ego kicks in, for example, where we want to be right or justify our point of view, we make it about 'us'. Our best quality thinking and sound judgement comes when we are not judging others.

Judith Glasser, an American Organisational Anthropologist, developed Conversational IQ. This is about communicating in a way that builds trust, integrity, empathy, and good judgment.

Her research revealed that being emotionally charged changes how we see and interpret reality and, therefore, how we talk about it. In addition, when we're fearful or upset, we lose the capacity to show empathy. In 2017, Google's 'Project Aristotle' determined what made its 'best' internal teams so successful. At the top of the list were a range of soft skills including empathy and emotional safety.

The reality is that across the Australian business landscape, people's needs are not being met, which is why engagement levels are so low. According to Gallup, less than a quarter (24%) of employees in Australia are engaged. Employee engagement has not budged in a decade and measuring engagement isn't sufficient to improve it. Leaders with whom I work, tell me they don't have the time to meet the needs of their team while they face increasing pressure to deliver more with less resources.

Research suggests that 75% of Australian employees want better leaders. We are disconnected, disparate and desperate for real leadership. Research from the Swinburne Leadership Institute (2014) revealed that Australian leaders care more about their own self-interest 75% of the time.

Never before has the need to 'work smarter' been more pressing, and for trust and accountability to rebuild through organisations.

GIVING OTHERS CERTAINTY, IN A POSITIVE WAY, COMES FROM A LEADER'S SENSE OF SELF-CERTAINTY.

You can only serve others first when you're not driven by the need to meet your needs first. The degree to which you can meet the needs of others first depends on how well you know and understand you and how self-aware you are.

Most people think they are self-aware—they aren't. Research shows only 10–15% of people are self-aware. As a result, many leaders think they are better leaders than what they are. [ix]

PEOPLE WHO LACK SELF-AWARENESS MAKE IT ABOUT THEM IN ORDER TO GAIN CONTROL.

What do you notice about people who aren't self-aware? One of the tell-tale signs is they make things about them. So when, for example, you share something with them, they will take a theme, idea, opinion from your story into their world and tell it from their perspective. All of a sudden, they have replaced your story with their own.

In the workplace, ego is one of the big giveaways of poor self-awareness. People show their ego by wanting to be right, having the last word, and justifying and rationalising their point of view without acknowledging someone else's.

I'm working with Penny. Penny's boss has 'talked up' a new female peer of Penny's, Amy. On Amy's first day, Penny invited her out for a coffee. Amy declined. Penny felt rejected; she retreated and decided she wasn't going to have the relationship with Amy that she'd expected. Amy appeared super confident and it left Penny feeling a little insecure and insignificant. When Penny realised she'd taken Amy's response personally, she was able to appreciate that 'no' on one day could mean 'yes' on another. She realised that her hasty reaction to 'decide' how things were with Amy had made her unable to see other choices that would have enabled her to be proactive in wanting to develop a relationship with Amy. Penny had fallen into the trap of 'making it all about her'. She also appreciated that Amy's over-confidence could be a front for feeling vulnerable in a new role.

People often make it about themselves to create certainty. However, our ego disconnects us from others, where it becomes harder to be empathetic and supportive. Ego and positive influence are negatively correlated.

As a leader you have to be emotionally aware
you have to deal with different types of people.
Being good at your job isn't good enough.
Often we miss a lot of signals, because we're
so tied up in ourselves. If we're tied up in ourselves,
we can't possible have the level of
emotional EQ we need.

—*Kylie Bishop*

PEOPLE WHO ARE SELF-AWARE
MAKE IT ABOUT OTHERS.
THEY GIVE UP THE NEED FOR CONTROL.

People who are self-aware are able to think about the context and the situation they are in, and react and respond in ways that considers others. As a result, they:

- think more resourcefully; they make better decisions and show less stress and anxiety
- communicate to have more influence
- develop better relationships
- become more politically savvy
- build a better personal brand
- experience greater satisfaction
- tap into resilience.

Self-awareness is the opportunity to look within and to see, understand, appreciate and accept what is already there within you. Self-awareness is the opportunity to redefine the relationship you have with you, and to understand and appreciate what is working and what is not; this will help create the self-certainty you need.

Internal self-awareness has two key parts:

1. Giving the gift of you: your listening, your presence, your empathy. All of these things allow someone else to be comfortable enough to be themselves.
2. Receiving the gift of you: to know, trust, value and love you. To know what drives you: your values and beliefs, aspirations and motivations, your strengths, your blind spots, your behaviours and decisions.

How often, as a leader, do you question how well you know yourself?

- What is driving my inner dialogue in how I talk to myself and treat myself?
- How can I improve the relationship I have with myself?
- How am I intentionally growing and developing? What is my proof?
- How do I motivate myself?
- Am I living in line with my values and principles consistently?
- Am I moving in the direction of what I want for my role/ life?

CAN YOU COUNT ON YOU?

Playing your big game starts with you. The heart of leadership is self-leadership. Leadership is a journey of self-improvement through your ability to self-reflect and see yourself from different perspectives.

Leadership is a privilege, not a right or a title. At the core of great leadership, is a belief that others can count on you. But can you count on you?

Are all of the people, who you think are following you as a leader, actually following you? If you're doubtful or you know it's a clear no, then you need to learn and understand more about you. Here are some things to explore about yourself:

- how you manage yourself
- how you keep the promises you make to yourself (to know you can trust you)
- how you back yourself
- the standards you set for yourself that you meet consistently.

YOU ARE UNIQUELY YOU. NO ONE CAN TELL YOU HOW TO BE YOU.

The holy grail of self-awareness is when your version of you (who you are for you) matches the external version of you (how others see you). In other words, who you are on the inside matches the outside. There is no 'trying' to look good by tailoring what you say and what you do to meet the needs, expectations, wants or desires of others. You're congruent with who you are and who you want to be. That's a life long journey for most people.

People want to connect in intrinsically through what matters to them. Our values represent the experiences we want to have.

I asked Tina to list, on a piece of paper, words that described what she cared about most at work. She listed the words learning, achievement, growth, and development. That all sounded good and polished (what she believed she needed to experience being the high performer she was). Later, in that coaching session, she discovered something that she valued just as much—playfulness (what she wanted to experience). Tina realised that by taking herself too seriously in pursuit of wanting to make her mark in her new role, she wasn't tapping into some of the deeper, more vulnerable areas of her personality that would allow her to experience being playful.

A recent HBR article, *What self-awareness really is (and how to cultivate it)*, describes an additional external lens of self-awareness, which is understanding how other people view us, in terms of those same factors listed above.

Self-awareness is the key to emotional intelligence, personal growth, confidence, and self-mastery.

YOUR ABILITY TO REACH YOUR POTENTIAL LIES WITH YOUR RELATIONSHIP WITH CERTAINTY.

On my self-development journey, I learnt what motivates me. The basis of this discovery was Anthony Robbins' 'Six Core Needs'. We have six core needs that we must meet. These needs are not just desires or wants, and we will only behave in ways that ensure we have those needs met.

Most of us are driven by certainty as one of our core needs. We want to feel in control, to be certain of ourselves and/ or our environment. Many of us are driven by comfort and predictability. It explains why, for example, we stay in a role we don't like and keep within our comfort zone. We love to feel in control; it helps us interpret and make sense of our world in a way that is predictable and safe.

The more certainty we seek, however, the less risks we take. We experience less growth and become more uncertain outside our comfort zone. How we ascertain certainty—through controlling others, through our ego (both are unresourceful ways of creating certainty), or through believing in ourselves (a resourceful way to create certainty)—determines the quality of our lives.

When we build self-certainty through accepting and believing in ourselves, the more we'll seek to learn and build confidence and self-worth in the process. Most people are looking for certainty within their external environment to have their needs met. This is because most of us are self-uncertain.

The more we seek certainty outside of ourselves, the more uncertainty we'll experience. The only thing we control is ourselves—everything else is uncertain. Our ability to handle uncertainty is directly proportional to how much success we'll experience in our careers. The more uncertainty we can deal with, the better leaders we will become.

Some leaders are like swans, they look graceful on the surface but are peddling hard underneath. Other leaders—with the same IQ and potential—seem to achieve the same results by taking things in their stride. What's the difference? Ultimately, it comes down to a leader's self-awareness and how they lead themselves based on their level of self-certainty and confidence. Self-certainty allows us to accept and back ourselves to handle whatever comes along. This concept is outlined fully in Chapter 4.

BEING AN EFFECTIVE LEADER MEANS BEING SELF-EFFECTIVE.

This is not a sexy 'set and forget' process. Being self-effective is a continual process of self-reflection and self-learning to build awareness and behavioural flexibility over time. Often, people don't want to do their own self-diagnosis and they then wonder why they are not able to impact, influence and inspire their team and colleagues. Great leaders are certain, self-certain and passionate. It's a winning combination, which is why followers want to follow them.

Great leaders practice self-reflection on a daily basis. Being a leader is not about being the leader when the going is good or easy, when the rules and boundaries are known, or just for one job or project. Being a leader is about always being a leader regardless of what is happening, what needs to be done and who is involved. Quality self-reflection is the most important thing in becoming more self-aware.

THE **JOURNEY** OF SELF-AWARENESS IS THE JOURNEY OF LEADERSHIP.

At the beginning of this chapter, I mentioned that leadership is a journey of personal discovery and growth, marked by stages of self-awareness. Leadership is not a tick in a box and there is no point of arrival. Learning leadership and the art of influence happens over a career. No career is a straight line. No one has a perfect or easy ride as they climb the career ladder. Just because you get a promotion doesn't mean you've 'made it' at the next level. Inherent in the journey is setback, challenge, failure, self-doubt and success: all of these are in equal measure. It's a continual process of self-evaluation and self-reflection. Each role has its own set of challenges.

As a leader, you will be judged by your results. More importantly, you'll be remembered for who you were for others.

LEADERSHIP IS A SPECTRUM WITH MILLIONS OF POINTS ON THE PATH.

I work with many people who believe they have grown to be better leaders than they actually are. A few years ago, I was working with Sally. She thought she was an inspirational leader. However, during our conversation she said, 'Toni, I know how to get people to get the job done'. Her language gave her away. Although she believed she was an inspirational leader, it was clear she worked with others by telling them what to do. When people don't know where their leadership is at, they can't see the next stage in what their leadership growth looks like or what they need to focus on. That is why I developed a *Stages of leadership model*. Let's look at the four stages in a leadership journey through the lens of self-awareness. There is a tipping point in the journey when the focus changes from self-focus to others-focus, which is the key stepping-stone into real leadership.

Your leadership career isn't marked by the titles or promotions you've had. It's marked by stages of your self-awareness that have allowed you to move from being a reactive leader to a proactive leader and have greater influence and impact. The following descriptions give greater insights into the distinctions between the levels of leadership.

REACTIVE LEADERSHIP

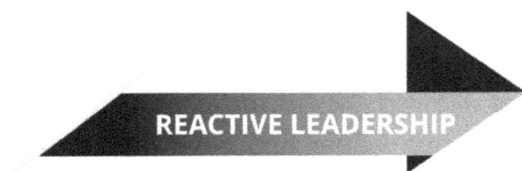

	DIRECTIVE LEADER	PERSONABLE LEADER
	Level 1 It's about me	**Level 2** It's about me and my team
Personal focus	Get more (self-focused)	Get less (self-focused)
Self-awareness	I'm unaware. I make judgements.	I'm curious about myself. I make judgements in context. I can adapt to change.
Leadership style	**Direct (tell)**	**Influence (tell)**
Leadership attitude	What's good for me is good for you. Being the boss.	What's good for us is good for me and you. Managing results through people.
Leadership focus	Get others to get the job done (manage).	Engage others (manage).
Strength of relationships	**Low trust. Low influence.**	**Patchy trust. Variable influence.**
Leadership brand	**Known for the title they have.**	**Known for what they know.**

PROACTIVE LEADERSHIP →

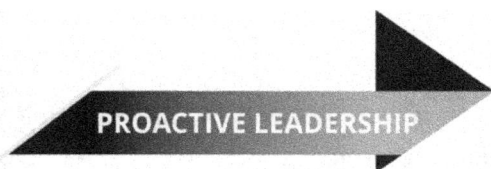

ACTION LEADER	LEGACY LEADER
Level 3 It's about my team	**Level 4** It's about others and my community
Give (others-focused)	Give more (others- focused)
I'm self-aware. I chose a perspective within a different context. I embrace uncertainty with optimism.	I'm self-certain and am becoming self-masterful. Life happens in flow (no attachment).
Develop (coach)	**Inspire (mentor)**
What's good for you is good for me. Leading change by creating a high performing environment.	What's good for everyone (not about self). Creating a legacy through developing others into their potential.
Empower others (lead).	Inspire others (lead).
Solid trust. **Solid influence.**	**High trust.** **High influence.**
Known for what they achieve.	**Known for who they are.**

LEVEL 1: DIRECTIVE LEADER

Directive leadership is where new, inexperienced leaders begin—usually through promotion. It is where the technician who can generate results is offered the opportunity to step up and lead team results.

Directive Leaders have little or no idea of how to manage and lead people. They want and hope people will do their jobs. As leaders, they believe they need to prove themselves so they make things all about them, which disconnects others around them.

What they do:

- They use their positional power to influence.
- They expect people to do as they are told.
- They rely on processes, rules, and bureaucracy to get work done: It's the way we do things around here.
- They 'tell' rather than 'show'.
- They notice what's not right and what's missing in team performance.
- They put their own needs before the teams.

The environment they create:

- They have no understanding of how they contribute to a lack of results and to the team environment/culture.
- Because Directive Leaders are about themselves, team members make it about themselves too. This creates a group of individuals, not a connected team.

The example they set:

- They demonstrate ego (the need to be right, justify, and get even). They don't have the self-awareness to know how to be different.
- They love positive feedback and take credit for great results, I've achieved this—even if it were a team effort. They pass the buck when things go wrong and play the blame game.
- They seek to be understood before they understand.
- Team results are reflective of the technical competence of team members.

Self-awareness is low.

Low accountability.

Low influence.

Low trust in the team.

Low team engagement and commitment.

How long someone stays at this level depends on the leadership role models around them and their organisation's commitment and investment into their leadership growth.

LEVEL 2: PERSONABLE LEADER

Personable leadership is where the leader begins to support, engage and influence people through genuine relationships and connection, not just position. They set the example others want to follow. When people feel liked, included, and valued they begin to work together—with their leader and each other. The whole working environment reflects this shift.

What they do:

- They position themselves as the go-to person in the team, potentially creating an overly high reliance on the leader and little empowerment of team members to act. (They typically have the right answer.)
- They refrain from having the hard/tough conversations, including team member feedback—they want to be liked.
- They support team members proactively, but when under pressure and stressed, their support can be patchy and directive (they revert to type—their dominant thinking patterns and behaviours that make it about them).
- They work within high 'busyness' in day-to-day implementation.

The environment they create:

- Results are achieved because everyone 'gets along' and gets the job done. There is appreciation of the team. Team morale is driven by how people 'feel' about being in the team, and the strength of relationships and team dynamics.

- The team maintains belief in the leader rather than belief in the overarching organisational mission and values.
- Team dynamics are based on the leader's EQ. For example, if the leader is at times moody (low EQ), the way the team work with the leader and each other will change as a function of people accommodating this leader's behaviour.

The example they set:

- A high leadership performance level is based on leveraging technical ability. The team revolves around the leader and the KPI's that need to be achieved.
- Results are dependent upon the results of the leader and within their ability to make effective decisions showing sound judgement.
- Leaders give praise but miss most opportunities to coach, mentor and develop team members.
- Team strengths are often the leader's strengths. Self-awareness is growing (as long as results are there).

Confidence growing/level
of connectedness growing.

Self-awareness growing.

Growing accountability.

Trust starting.

Team engagement and commitment
is improving/positive.

Team performance is growing.

LEVEL 3: ACTION LEADER

Action leadership is where the leader sets the example, and others are engaged and motivated to follow to achieve great results. The leader is a visible and trusted high performer who can connect effectively through the organisation to engage and influence.

What they do:

- They set the direction of the team.
- They effectively engage and influence to push the team. The leader's performance means the team can step up its own performance and set the standard for everyone else.
- They challenge the status quo.
- They encourage creativity and opportunity to improve and expand core business to grow their market position.
- They think critically and see a bigger picture.
- They focus on the goals that matter and discern what's important.
- They achieve great results, which builds their credibility and reputation.
- They give useful feedback; however, this can misfire or be misinterpreted depending on the leaders EQ.
- They develop others based on their own strengths and can miss training/mentoring coaching opportunities/gaps across the team.

The environment they create:

- They create an energy and buzz that people want to be part of.
- People want to connect in and join the team.
- Momentum is the team is building.
- There is a high-performance team environment (a high learning environment when there is openness and transparency). There are genuine connections based on trust.
- There is a high reliance on the leader's performance.

The example they set:

- They make an impact on the organisation and others around them. Great results are expected but the focus is on how the results are achieved. Action leaders believe they are the change they wish to see in others. They appreciate that they set the tone for others to follow.
- They are a positive leadership role model who makes progress over and above the day-to-day execution. They look to optimise and innovate through creating new challenge benchmarks for achieving KPI's.

They have high self-awareness.
(They embrace uncertainty.)

There is high credibility.

Building a high-performing team.

Med–high influence.

Trust is building.

There is high engagement and commitment in the team.

They attract great people who believe what they do.

They create an environment where people feel
they belong and find meaning.

Team performance is high.

LEVEL 4: LEGACY LEADER

Legacy leadership is where the core focus moves from achieving team results to developing other leaders. This is the primary goal of all ambitious leaders keen to demonstrate their growth, contribution and abilities within their organisation. Leaders can become legacy leaders once they've achieved very senior leadership positions where the focus is less on results and more on developing the leaders beneath them.

What they do:

- They create the strategic direction.
- They refresh and reset how the organisation thinks and views itself.
- They believe in their team.
- They live their values and uphold their standards without exception.
- They share themselves authentically. They understand the value in being humble.
- They rely positively on their own abilities.
- They create opportunity for others to step up.
- They develop others through coaching and mentoring.
- They set the standard for how others engage with them based on their standards.
- They are clear about what success means for them, the team and individually.
- They align leadership teams on where they need to be.
- They develop critical and strategic thinking in others.
- They focus on the future and think inductively: what's the new game vs. what's a better game.

The environment they create:

- The high-performing team is fiercely loyal and gives 100% consistently. People are empowered to step up. They are inspired to improve in an environment where people are supported to excel and realise their potential.

The example they set:

- It's more than results. It's about the journey and ensuring everyone is engaged and inspired to bring their best. It's about putting people first.

There is high self-awareness
(others focused).

There is high confidence.

There is high accountability
(it's always me).

There is a high-performance culture.

There is high trust.

Inspires team/team members about
what's possible for them.

Leaders believe in the team/
the team believes in itself.

Leader knows how to
develop the team.

AT THE HEART OF SELF-AWARENESS IS SELF-ACCEPTANCE.

At the heart of the self-awareness journey is to see yourself accurately and to see yourself as whole and complete. If you don't accept you exactly as you are, you'll always be looking for validation from others. You'll care too much about what other people think of you, and you'll work too hard and stretch yourself too thin trying to be good enough for everyone. It's exhausting. I work with clients who believe, when we peel all the layers away, that something is wrong with them. While they don't express in these exact words, it is what they believe deep down.

We will explore this in much more detail in the next chapter when we tap into the resources you'll need to help you succeed. The rest of this book will show you how to move from self-focus to others-focus, so you can step into the next chapter of your leadership journey.

The greatest gift we can give ourselves is to accept ourselves as whole and complete, exactly the way we are.

CHAPTER 4

SELF-CERTAINTY DRIVES CONFIDENCE

CONFIDENCE AND INFLUENCE GO HAND IN HAND.

It's clear that confidence matters. Confidence means you speak up, step out, and stand up in a way you're heard so that you can achieve your goals, find happiness and—as much as possible—lead a stress free life. As Katty Kay and Claire Shipman wrote in *The Confidence Code*, 'Confidence is hard to define but easy to recognize. With it, you can take on the world; without it, you live stuck at the starting block of your potential'.

You're not born confident or non-confident. Confidence is an external representation of your inner self-certainty.

Confidence is knowing you can do something.
Self-confidence is knowing you are fine if you can't.

—Julian Short

Often, the perceptions others have of us are more accurate than the perceptions we have of ourselves. We move through our day doing our best to get it right, to look good, and to be perceived well. However, what underlies this way of being is the fear created through a lack of self-esteem. Fear stops us from pursuing what we want and from being our true selves.

We fear that it won't work, that we'll get rejected. We fear that we will fail, and that we don't have what it takes. Fear is universal. Feeling self-doubt is normal. Before Gail Kelly, former Westpac CEO started a new role, she'd ask herself: What if I fail?

We're all worried that we're not good enough, and we get stuck when fear grows bigger than our courage.

> **Believe it when people can tell you can do it, even when you don't think you can. Nothing is impossible. The reward for the solution is more problems to solve. That's good for my brain muscles. That's exciting. That overrides any self-doubt. You look back in reflection and things that seemed hard weren't that hard. We are too harsh on ourselves in what we tell ourselves. We want to be perfect. Perfect is a killer word. No one is perfect. Accept that being 7–8/10 is okay or even 1/10 is okay, because that's you. You are where you're at. Sometimes the imperfectness gives you motivation and drive to do more. Do better. You accept what you are prepared to accept about yourself. Accept where you are and focus on the progress you can make.**
>
> —*Alice Wong*

CONFIDENCE ISN'T THE ABSENCE OF FEAR, IT'S TAKING ACTION IN THE FACE OF FEAR.

The only way to overcome fear is to let courage show up. Courage enables you to think differently, to get out of your comfort zone and back yourself to do the things of which you are afraid. If you wait for confidence to show up or for fear to subside, you'll be waiting for a long time, and your fear will grow bigger, rather than smaller.

Thought Leader Dr Sean Richardson said that success, as a strategy, is simple. You come up with a goal, define that goal in terms of what achieving it looks like compared to the current state, and then you do what it takes to achieve it. Simple, right?

While success, as a strategy, seems simple, we are not. People are complex. I spent my 20s and 30s climbing the corporate career ladder. My career was my life. I frequently compared myself to others, and tried to hide my flaws. I was always trying to measure up, and it was stressful and exhausting. Then, shortly after I started working for ANZ, I was invited to a divisional strategy offsite day. I was the junior in the room. At one point, we broke up into small discussion groups and when we regrouped, I was invited to address the room on behalf of my group. As I moved to the front of the room, I could feel myself being consumed with fear. I couldn't remember the topic we had discussed, let alone any relevant insight or discussion points. My mind went blank. As I turned to face everyone, I froze. They looked at me. I looked at them. It was the longest minute of my life. I could see my boss laughing with the guy next to him (I didn't realise at the time that they were sharing a joke—completely unrelated to me), and it made me feel more humiliated. All I could think about was running out the door and never coming back to my job. I knew I couldn't do that though. What I subsequently learned about the fight, flight or freeze response is that the freeze response occurs when you decide (subconsciously) that there is no hope for you in what you are about to do. Eventually I found my voice and got through it. That incident was a lesson for me, and the lesson was to see the relationship I had with myself. My strategy for coping with fear was to prepare and rehearse to 'get it right' and to 'look good'. It gave me a transactional sense of confidence and control. Without that strategy, there was only fear. And up there, facing the entire room, my fear of being judged was far greater than my capacity to back myself. Underpinning my fear was my imposter syndrome, my self-belief that I'm not good enough.

WE JUDGE OTHERS BY WHAT THEY HAVE. WE JUDGE OURSELVES BY WHAT WE PERCEIVE WE LACK.

This jolt made me appreciate I wasn't as self-aware or as confident as I believed. I thought I had it together. There were plenty of times I'd backed myself and achieved. I was a high achiever and had the résumé to prove it.

The reality is, when we put ourselves out there, our relationships with fear and uncertainty will be tested. Even now, when I think I have a good enough handle on my I'm not good enough belief, there are days when I don't feel confident. It can be hard to remember moments of positivity when I feel self-doubt, when I feel like an imposter, or when I'm sure I won't ever quite measure up to the amazing success of the other women entrepreneurs I watch and admire.

Your success, however you define it, will always start with the relationship you have with you. In turn, it will drive every other relationship you have.

WHAT DOES SUCCESS MEAN TO YOU?

We grow up believing society's view of success—money, house, car, holidays, highly paid roles, promotions—matters most. The premise is that once I'm successful, then I'll be happy. Success that comes from 'getting' is a trap because it's short lived. Eventually, the pursuit of proving ourselves becomes exhausting. We become disillusioned, and we question what it's all for. In other words, 'getting stuff' as the benchmark for success will only lead to more unhappiness. No one else can define what you want and what your success looks like. Your path doesn't need to make sense to anyone but you. Your benchmarks for success must be your own.

Sally Capp became Melbourne's Lord Mayor this year. Sally was one of the senior executives I interviewed for this book. She commented that other people, at various points in her career, questioned her career choices. In Sally's mind, her career choices were well considered and congruent with the experiences she wanted to gain in each role. Others didn't need to make sense of her journey—to Sally her choices made perfect sense. I admired her confidence in running her race her way, and I think there's a lesson for us all in that.

The more we search for success outside of ourselves, the further away we find it. Our success is to heal ourselves first. The biggest gift we can afford ourselves is to accept ourselves as we are right now.

I've just begun working with a client who's moved from Melbourne to Sydney to start a new role. When I quizzed her on what this life transition offered her, she told me she wanted to reinvent herself. New opportunities are exciting. Whether it's a new role, new relationship, new city or country or new group to join; we hope the grass will be greener on the other side. Have you ever, though, stepped into something new and faced the same underlying challenges or issues? For my new client, 'reinventing' herself will come through the change she's willing to create from within herself. The new city and the new job is simply a catalyst for doing this work.

CHANGING YOUR ENVIRONMENT WILL NOT CHANGE YOU.

Get curious about your relationship with yourself, it's currently defining how you experience your entire world. I left a physically and emotionally abusive marriage when I was 31. I believed my next relationship would be different, that I wouldn't make the same mistakes and that I'd never be mistreated again. I was wrong. I did get treated like that again. My next significant relationship was also dysfunctional and emotionally abusive. How could I have let that happen? It wasn't bad luck. It was a pattern. I could look back to many relationships (in my personal and professional life) where I put others' needs above my own, was too accommodating, and didn't say what I wanted. I didn't realise that the quality of my relationships was simply a reflection of the quality of the relationship I had with myself—poor. My inability to have my needs met and create boundaries for myself: how I wanted to be spoken to and how I wanted to be treated and heard, meant I was treated however someone wanted to treat me. Blaming others wasn't the answer. The change had to start with me, and that journey had to start right back at the beginning with my belief that I wasn't good enough.

Shame is the most powerful, master emotion.
It tells us we're not good enough.

—Brené Brown

In focusing on 'getting' and 'fixing', we forget we are whole. We believe we are unworthy. So we hide behind 'stuff' and 'busyness' because we don't know how to fill the void within us (refer to Figure 2 further on in this chapter, which graphically represents this choice, as a way of being, that lies between who we are and who we want to be). We all carry shame about our failures, our mistakes, times when we've let ourselves down, and when we thought we were not enough. We think the past is our future and we become trapped.

Most of us are looking for salvation—the hope of a second chance—where our life will be different. Better. Fixed. We'll have the fulfilling life that we desire, and along the way, we'll set ourselves free and become the person we're meant to be, where finally, we're good enough. The reality is that most people need to find themselves, let alone create themselves. Most people don't know that they have the power to decide who and what they want to be.

YOU CAN'T 'LEARN' OR 'GET' AUTHENTICITY, YOU NEED TO TAP INTO 'YOU'.

You can't prepare to be you. You can't try to be you. In order to be you, you just have to be you. The degree to which you are trying to be you, is the degree to which people don't know the real you. People want to connect with the real you.

> **When I joined 2Mobile in the UK as Retail Director, my predecessor (Russell) was dynamic, amazing and well loved; he could do no wrong. I spent my first 3–4 months shadowing him. When he left, I spent the next six months trying to be him. It was the only thing I could do to gain credibility and success. I had no idea who I was. I used the same language and mannerisms as he did. It took two colleagues, with real courage, to say to me, We have no idea who you are. Just be who you really are. Be the leader you are. Be the person you are. Trust yourself enough to be vulnerable and reveal who you are. We want you for who you are. That was one of the most important lessons of my leadership journey.**
>
> —*John Coull*

Your authentic self comes from your values. Leadership is not about being perfect. It's about being effective and congruent with your values and beliefs—every single day.

Being authentic feels good. You know when you are being authentic and when you're not. There is a bigger, bolder, braver, more real version of you waiting to surface.

Today, people want leaders who are real, grounded, open, transparent and vulnerable. With such leaders, there's no BS, ego, jargon or hidden agendas. Real leaders know how to connect and relate to others. They are humble. Humble leaders show sides of themselves with which we can all connect. Roger Federer welled up when he won his 20th Grand Slam in Melbourne in January 2018. His tears showed us what the win meant to him, 'I'm so happy, it's unbelievable. Winning is an absolute dream come true'. His ability to show emotion enabled us to connect to that emotion in a way that helps celebrate someone's success.

At the core of the authenticity challenge is how we grapple with our fear of not being worthy or good enough. That is, how can we be authentic when we fear being found out as not good enough? As a fraud?

WHY IS BEING YOURSELF SO HARD?

For starters, we want to be liked. We want to belong. We want to be bulletproof. We want to be seen to be doing the 'right' things. We fear being judged. Yet the people judging us are ourselves. We judge ourselves on the idea that we need to show we can do it all. That we can balance multiple demands for our time: career, parenthood, kids' activities, friends, aging parents, family etc. We stretch ourselves because we want to 'look good'. We want it to look easy, like we've got it all together. Anything else shows we're not good enough. We're afraid of being found out to be less than what we want others to perceive us to be. This is terrifying for some people.

At the base of our ego are three universal fears:

- not being good enough
- not belonging
- not being loved.

Our ego is a self-protection mechanism that aims to keep us safe by limiting us to our comfort zone. For example, our ego drives our need to be right, to justify, and to judge others in a way that makes us feel better about ourselves.

Why do women tend to apologise more than men? We develop language patterns in our formative years. According to Deloitte Digital's, *Women at Work* podcast, if you look at how girls and boys play in same sex groups, the differences are stark.[x] For example, when girls play together, girls who 'talk themselves up' are criticised as being 'bossy'. The implication is that girls then learn to minimise themselves. Boys, on the other hand, tend to lean toward rough and tumble play and play fighting, and they're more comfortable talking about what they are good at.

How do these traits play out at work? Women tend to talk in ways that downplay their authority. For example, a female might say to her direct report 'Sorry to interrupt, can you do this for me?' compared to a male counterpart who is more likely to make the request directly. Men tend to challenge, debate and explore ideas, and be more comfortable with conflict. The podcast summarises that women are socialised to be less confident as well as sound less confident.

DO YOU PUT YOURSELF DOWN TOO EASILY?

The podcast also outlined Laurie Hetherington's research where first-year female students chose to make their academic grade expectations either public or hidden. Results showed that women who made their expectations public predicted lower grades. In other words, they downplayed what grade they expected so they wouldn't come across as boastful or 'too full of themselves'. This finding rang true in my own experience at university. I downplayed what I wanted to achieve in my exams and final grades in case I scored lower. Doubting myself to lose was easier than doubting myself to win.

YOU CAN STILL SUCCEED WITH LOW CONFIDENCE AND SELF-ESTEEM, BUT IT COMES AT A COST, AND YOU'LL ONLY GO SO FAR.

A client, Sam, was offered an external job role as a consultant. Although he considered the role a fantastic opportunity to develop and do work he loved, he turned it down. He doubted his ability to transfer his knowledge and skills successfully to a consultancy role. While he rationally justified his decision around the salary not being sufficient, deep down, I believe he decided to play it safe. His self-doubt drove his decision not to accept the role. A decision, I'm thinking, he will regret.

Be careful how you talk to yourself because you are listening.

—Lisa M Hayes

Your inner voice is the relationship you have with you. You're always listening to the voice in your head. You know the one. When it's negative; it tells you that you can't do something or that you haven't done the right thing. It tells you that you haven't done enough or that it's safer to go with the flow and say nothing.

The cost of low confidence is influence. Sue contacted me at a crossroads. She was about to return from maternity leave and believed she deserved a promotion as she was coming back as part of a wider restructure. Her results were great. However, she realised she'd fallen into the trap of believing her results would speak for themselves. She began to understand that she didn't have the relationships across her peer group and more senior leaders. Staying under the radar had kept her safe but it hadn't positioned her to get a tap on the shoulder. She didn't have the level of influence she needed to be seen as ready to problem solve and collaborate at the next level. The leadership lesson here is that your results won't speak for themselves, you must have a voice and proactively position your potential.

If you are like most people, you are your own worst critic. It's easier to judge and criticise yourself than to praise and acknowledge yourself. While the intentions of your inner voice are positive—to keep you safe in your comfort zone— your inner voice also holds you back. By over-thinking and over-analysing, you create drama, overwhelm and, in many cases, inaction.

ARE YOU A PERFECTIONIST?

I work with lots of people who are self-confessed perfectionists. While they recognise this in themselves and want to create change, they acknowledge it's been the source of their motivation, persistence, and hard work. They don't know to achieve without their perfectionism habit.

Perfectionism goes hand-in-hand with the fear of not being good enough.

A recent HBR article mentioned the energy behind perfectionism coming from the desire to avoid failure. The fear being, that if they fail, they'll expose some inner weakness or frailty.[xi]

There's nothing wrong with wanting to get things right and having high standards. Everyone has standards in operation for every facet of their lives. Standards are simply a set of behaviours built upon expectations you have of yourself in a variety of situations. They're your own set of rules for how you live and how you treat others. High standards set the benchmark for what you want to achieve and how you want to achieve it. In other words, they help you define who you need to be and what you need to bring consistently so that you can achieve what you want. Standards help you not put up with excuses. Instead, they help make you accountable. They help you bring your values and goals to life. They are, in some respects, performance standards.

Think about the standards athletes have around their diet, fitness and training regime. High performers have high standards. Their standards are reflected in choices they make, how they behave, and how they show up for others. However, your standards are not about trying to be perfect. If you're a perfectionist, you will always create a gap between what you did or the result you achieved and how it could have been or should have been. The gap defines what wasn't good enough and represents your judgement of you or your perception of how others are judging you (which is actually you judging you).

Perfectionists validate their belief that they are not good enough through the habit of perfectionism. It's a vicious cycle of self-talk that has people continually self-doubt themselves and judge themselves.

There's no such thing as perfect.
Chasing perfect is the shortest road to not achieving it.

—*Gary Vaynerchuk*

Perfectionists believe they have high standards. It often comes as a surprise when I tell them they have no standards. In always creating the gap, there is never a standard to attain. The way to break the habit of perfectionism is to shift the focus to the effort made, what is being learned, and what progress is being achieved. In other words, taking the focus away from the negative judgement of the result or outcome as it relates to self to positively acknowledging the contribution being made.

SELF-CERTAINTY AND INFLUENCE ARE A PARTNERSHIP.

The biggest gift you can give yourself is to stop judging the leader you were and focus on the leader you want to become. This comes from having a strong sense of self and being able to know you, accept you, care for you and value your worth. When you know who you are, you can show up as you. You are more grounded and centred. People don't have to guess who you are or wonder how you're going to react. People know what to expect from you. They know how you will show up because you show up consistently.

AS LEADERS, WHEN WE ARE NOT SELF-CERTAIN, WE LOOK FOR CERTAINTY OUTSIDE OF OURSELVES.

By judging ourselves, we create layers around ourselves of who we believe we need to be versus who we really are. The gap in between is how we experience our leadership. The diagram below shows a graphical representation of this.

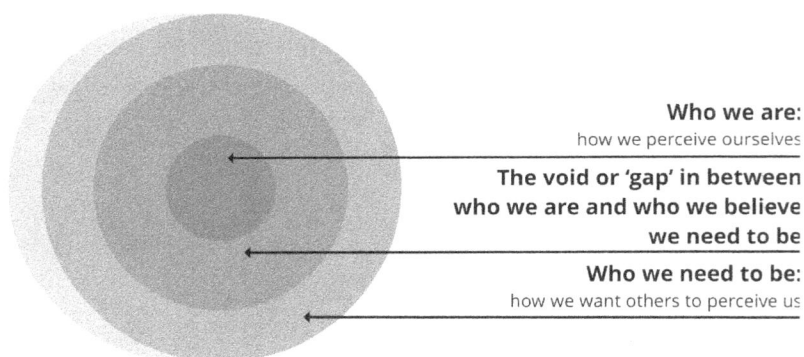

Who we are:
how we perceive ourselves

The void or 'gap' in between who we are and who we believe we need to be

Who we need to be:
how we want others to perceive us

FIGURE 2: SELF-PERCEPTION MODEL

Our self-esteem—our sense of personal value and worth— relies on validation from others and creates the perception of how we want others to see us (the outer circle). The inner circle captures what we really believe about ourselves and is fuelled by our limiting beliefs—the primary one: 'I'm not good enough'. We protect this circle so that we're not discovered as frauds. The space in the middle is the void. This is the gap between who we are and who we believe we need to be.

I've shared this diagram with many of my clients who, although being confronted by it, begin to appreciate this is the construct in which they've lived their lives: doing the right thing, meeting the expectations of others, pleasing others, putting the needs of others above our own, doing well, getting ahead, and achieving (which creates the outer circle). All of these things have given them positive validation from others, with the underlying purpose of being seen as 'good enough', because what they fear the most is being found out as not being good enough, which is the overarching core negative belief in the inner circle. It is for this reason that people with low self-esteem find getting critical feedback so challenging; it jeopardises the outer circle when there's a risk 'they've been found out' as being less than what they really are.

My clients also appreciate that creating this circle of validation has fuelled their motivation, as their core strategy to succeed. Yes, I tell them, but at what cost? Keeping their outer circle intact is stressful and time-consuming.

Mel was a high achieving Head of Operations in a large corporate and aspired to a General Management role as her next career step. She knew she was capable, had a great personal brand, and her team loved working with her. However, she was well on the way to burnout and she knew it. Why? As a self-confessed perfectionist, she negatively compared herself to her peers. She over-analysed situations and judged herself harshly at every turn. Afraid of being found out as a fraud, she believed she needed to go above and beyond the expectations she perceived others had of her (keeping the outer circle intact), while never meeting her own, which in turn, validated her 'I'm not good enough' belief (keeping her inner circle intact).

YOU HAVE TO BELIEVE THAT YOU ARE GOOD ENOUGH.

The starting point for Mel was for her to believe she was enough, to accept herself as she was. While she rationally knew she was good enough, she didn't believe it. Therefore, she connected emotionally into this in a way she 'got it'. She created and validated new self-beliefs while learning to back herself. In addition, she created resourceful personal standards, letting go of her perfectionism habits. She created a new relationship with herself and in the process, became a more intentional and influential leader.

Decide that you are enough. Stop wanting to please other people.

SELF-CERTAINTY IS THE ROAD TO SELF-ACCEPTANCE AND SELF-BELIEF.

When we are self-certain, we no longer need to look outside of ourselves for certainty, validation or control. We don't crave positive feedback (that tells us we're good enough), nor do we need to rate being liked above saying what needs to be said (that tells us we belong). We don't need to create an 'outer circle'. In other words, when no longer have to rely on a strategy we can't control—we take back our power.

There is nothing to 'get' outside of you to 'fix' you. As I keep saying, your success is the day you remember you have everything you need within you. You just need to access it. Your power comes from understanding you and accepting you as you are. No one is perfect. Everyone has their unique combination of strengths and stretches.

When you are self-uncertain your sense of self is vastly different from who you believe you are for others. When you are self-certain your sense of self matches who you are for others.

YOUR LEADERSHIP IS YOUR ABILITY TO
BELIEVE IN YOU, TO KNOW YOU, TO TRUST YOU,
AND TO VALUE YOU. IF YOU CAN'T GIVE THOSE
THINGS TO YOURSELF, YOU CAN'T
GIVE THEM TO OTHERS.

Don't invest in looking good. Invest instead in being better. There's a very big difference between arrogance and a strong sense of self. Arrogance presents itself with a lack of maturity. The key is to stay vulnerable but strong. I never really thought about leadership. I was a reluctant leader who was great at the 'people' side of things. People skills came naturally to me. I once entered a talent program. I had a coach who watched me in every interaction. We did a simulation exercise, which I was good at. But the coach said to me, 'you do what you do, and it comes easy to you, but you're not being intentional about it and it's an absolute disservice to those who choose to work with and for you. Those words will always ring in my ears. I fought the feedback, but I knew it was true. It was like I'd never really spent time thinking about it. The way that translated was that I'd never really taken the space to say, hey, I can play a leadership role here. I would always do it in the background. So, from that day, I've been much more intentional about it. I used to have all these beautiful connotations of what I thought a people leader should be. I've dropped all those. I simply want to be a consistent people leader with high integrity. That's it. People know what they're going to get with me regardless of whether it's a good or bad day. Inconsistency is just poor leadership. It's not the right way to be.

—Kylie Bishop

WHEN YOU ARE SELF-CERTAIN:

People don't have to approve of you.

People don't have to like you or your opinions.

People don't have to validate you.

You embrace opportunity and take risks.

You say what needs to be said without fear of judgement.

You don't put yourself down in order to be positively validated by others.

You view you needs as being equal to others.

You have boundaries and ensure they are respected.

You know your own benchmarks for success.

You can be spontaneous.

You can be vulnerable.

You live by your values.

You back you.

You look after you.

(content attribution: The Coaching Institute).

BECOMING A SELF-CERTAIN LEADER.

There are three interconnected keys to becoming self-certain.

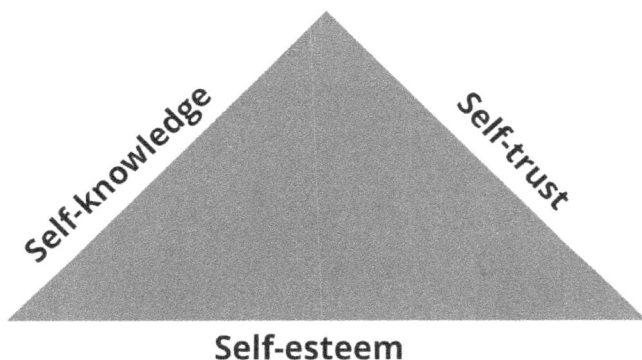

FIGURE 3: BUILDING SELF-CERTAINTY MODEL

Build self-knowledge: This is being able to show up as you are and act with integrity according to your principles and values. Be clear on who you are for you and what you believe about you. Connect in to what is important to you and what you love to do.

When I started in my own business, I frequently asked myself: Who am I to go from being a corporate marketer to a leadership expert? It's taken me a while to feel comfortable with that. At the time, I didn't appreciate that I had placed rules on myself that limited me, for example, I couldn't call myself an expert unless I'd achieved a certain level of success. I then realised I could define myself within my new career path however I liked and that there was no right or wrong answer. That gave me the freedom to focus instead on the following beliefs:

- I believe in my ability to succeed.
- I earn my success through what I'm prepared to do.
- I can add massive value to the people I coach and train.
- I am worthy of my career success and the person I'm becoming.

Confidence is not based on your actual ability to succeed at a task but your belief in your ability to succeed.

Understand what matters the most to you. When you show up in line with what you value and care about, it'll be far easier to be you and others will 'get' you too.

Develop self-trust: This is your ability to back yourself and tell yourself, I've got this. Know your strengths and stretches (weaknesses). Like those you're leading, you have progress to make too. There is only progress to be made. This is the secret to you being you. Know that you are good enough and that you can reach the next level, however you define that for yourself.

Create opportunities to back yourself to develop your self-trust muscle by following the process below. Realise that you're only ever doing your best. You don't get up in the morning and think to yourself, I'm going to stuff it all up today. You can trust that you are going to give it your best. It's all you can expect of yourself and you can trust in that. Regardless of your competence level, your attitude is your choice. Bring an open attitude then regardless of the result, you'll take something away from the experience that is positive for you.

- Get out of your comfort zone.
- At the point of feeling alarm (fear), decide to back yourself and let courage show up.
- Bring a positive attitude and be ready to learn regardless of your competency level.
- Acknowledge yourself to lift you up (rather than bring you down).
- Keep on developing new reference points to know you can back yourself again and again.

Have solid self-esteem: This is the value you place in your own abilities and worth. The fastest way to build your self-worth is to keep the promises you make for yourself. Each time you make a commitment and don't keep it (for example, I wanted to go to the gym after work but I felt too tired to go so I went home instead) you lose a little bit of self-worth. If you can't trust your word, why should others?

The little voice in your head is you, so treat it with care and respect. It's not about shutting it down, it's about quietening it and refocusing, so you can step forward in the way you want.

I am imperfect and vulnerable and sometimes afraid, but that doesn't change the truth that I am also brave and worthy of love and belonging.

—*Brené Brown, The Gifts of Imperfection*

ACTIONS CREATE CONFIDENCE.

Confidence is not a fixed attribute; it's the outcome of the thoughts we think and the actions we take. No more, no less.

The actions of confidence come first, the feelings of confidence come later. Your confidence is linked to your preparedness to take action. You can't wish, wait and hope for confidence to show up. It won't. There is no 'ready' feeling. You can't read a book about confidence and expect to have it. Confidence isn't needed when we're thinking about it, it's needed when we're in it.

Alex Malley, author of *The Naked CEO* said, 'The only way to build self-confidence is to take a risk and take action despite your fear of failure, messing up or embarrassment. If things work out, then you now know you can do more than you think. If things don't work out, you now know that you can handle more than you think. Either way, you're better off.

YOU CAN BUILD SELF-CERTAINTY. YOU CAN HAVE THE CONFIDENCE YOU DESIRE.

You can change how you think. Research has now shown that our brains are 'plastic' and can be adapted and changed, forging new neural pathways according to how we stimulate and use them. This ability is called neuroplasticity and means we can change the physical structure of the brain to rewire our responses to challenges and improve our behaviours.

If you want something to change, then the change needs to start with you. You have to be willing to change how you see yourself, the thinking patterns and behavioural habits that have created your status quo. So if, up until now, you have dreaded opportunities to lean in and speak up or have let your self-doubt get the better of you, know that developing the confidence you want is now a conscious choice.

Dr Russ Harris's book, *The Confidence Gap* outlines the golden rule of the confidence game: 'You can't fake confidence, you have to earn it. You have to do the work'.

Developing self-certainty leads (on the inside) to experiencing confidence (in how you show up for others on the outside). The more confident you feel, the more you will speak up and have a voice—you can't have influence without it. Your ability to 'get over yourself' so that you can focus on the opportunity or the challenge by working effectively with and through others is critical. The relationship you have with yourself drives the quality and strength of the relationships you have with others. Let's now move into your relationships with others in the next chapter.

2

CONNECT INTO **OTHERS**

WHO AM I BEING FOR OTHERS?

CHAPTER 5:

RELATIONSHIPS: HOW MUCH DO YOU CARE?

YOU CAN INCREASE YOUR INFLUENCE
BY BECOMING A 360 LEADER.

At the beginning of a coaching relationship, I ask my clients what they'd like to achieve from us working together. A common objective is to increase leadership influence. If we go on to have a session exploring, for example, communication strategies to take the lead in conversations to influence others, I always start the session by talking about relationships. Why? Often, influencing isn't about the idea, the logic or the tactics, it's about the connections and the strength of relationships you have with others. Relationships are a precursor to influence. The better your relationships are, the more influence you will have.

Are your relationships as good as you think? What are you intentionally investing into your relationships?

Our relationships at work will help us achieve our goals and enable us to make a meaningful contribution. Our attitude goes a long way in building and establishing relationships. One example of this is acknowledging how much there is to learn from others who are lower on the chain of command; it's about receiving as well as giving in the form of providing support, mentoring and coaching.

People assume that senior people are where you need to network. That is flawed thinking. Your networking needs to be up, down, and sideways. It's not about looking good, it's about becoming better.

—Carlos Schafer

Think about the strength of your relationships with your peers up, down and across the leadership ladder: Where are your relationships the strongest? Where are they the weakest? What relationships would benefit from more investment to help you build the influence you would like to have?

To help you answer these questions, refer to the *Relationship heat map*. Think about where the strategic importance of your relationships is medium to high and the current state of your relationship is medium to low. This is where your 'low hanging fruit' is for where you can begin to build your relationships.

Please note that the strategic importance of the relationship might be attributable to, for example, someone being a key influencer, potential mentor, key stakeholder, career sponsor etc.

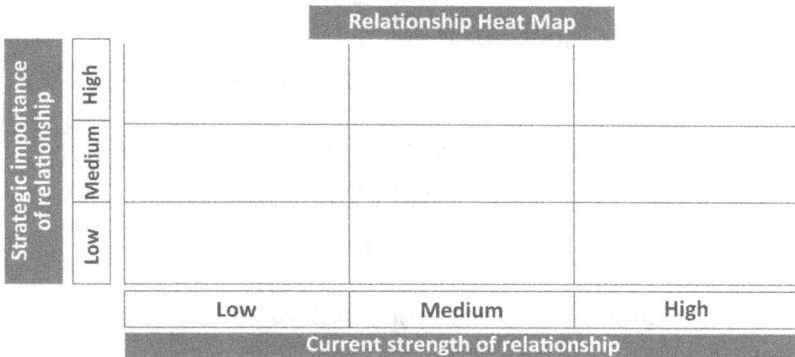

FIGURE 4: RELATIONSHIP HEAT MAP

YOUR RELATIONSHIPS DRIVE YOUR CAREER SUCCESS.

According to multiple research studies, simply being in an open network instead of a closed one is the best predictor of career success. In fact, one study revealed that half of the predicted difference in career success (promotion, pay, and industry recognition) is due to this one variable. [xii]

Forming open networks allows you to gain and share ideas and information that expand, challenge and adapt your thinking, and create new perspectives, insights and knowledge. By building open networks you are open to forming new connections and relationships.

We'd all love to have perfect relationships. Where we do what we want, when we want, exactly the way we want it. Wouldn't it be wonderful if others thought the way we did? Wonderful and boring. Instead, we have many diverse relationships. Some are effortless and some are plain hard work. We all have a way of developing relationships and working with others. We all have a comfort zone in our relationships.

> **In life you don't attract what you want,**
> **you attract what you are.**
>
> —*Joe Pane*

A mentor once said to me 'You don't have to like everyone, but you have to know how to work with everyone'. Think about your challenging relationships and ask yourself these questions: What are the dynamics that have created the relationship? How have you contributed to why the relationship is this way? What have you given to those relationships? What have you taken from them? These questions will give you some clues to how you can create the changes you want. Resetting any relationship starts with an open, honest conversation and laying the standards for how it can work effectively. With these ground rules in place, there is then a basis for providing feedback to each other, where you can hold each other accountable for making the relationship work and succeed together.

WHEN OTHERS CARE ABOUT US, WE EXPERIENCE BELONGING AND CONNECTION, WHICH IS WHAT WE WANT TO FEEL MORE THAN ANYTHING.

People want to feel appreciated and valued. They experience that by you demonstrating how much you care. That's what they want from you most—to know you care.

On average, we spend 46 years at work—90,000 hours— longer than most marriages. Therefore, a fulfilling life means having a fulfilling career. You can't have dysfunctional relationships at work and expect to be happy. Through relationships, we leverage the diversity across the people with whom we work; we connect into ideas and information; we build greater influence and lead change more effectively; we achieve more; and we become more engaged and satisfied. We also build our leadership brand that positions us for future opportunities. In other words, our relationships allow us to become more. Relationships fuel our ability to grow and contribute meaningfully within every facet of our lives.

The greatest ability in business is to get along with others and to influence their actions.

—*John Hancock (1737–1793)*

OUR WORLD IS RAPIDLY CHANGING.
THE BUSINESS LANDSCAPE IS TOO.

The scale of organisational change, market challenges, and accelerating speed of innovation are demanding new approaches to leadership and change. The ways in which we work together are creating new rules for how to work with and through others to achieve results.

According to the World Economic Forum's, *Future of Jobs* report, an estimated five million jobs will be lost to automation by 2020.[xiii] The report also predicts two thirds of children entering primary school today will end up working in industries and job types that don't exist yet. The Foundation for Young Australians released a report last year predicting that today's 15-year-olds will have 17 changes of employers across five different careers.

It's staggering to contemplate what the future holds for our children, and what it means for us and our roles right now. What's the biggest driver of this change? Artificial Intelligence and technology play a big part, but there are other reasons.

The *Tomorrow's Digitally Enabled Workforce* report released by the Government in 2017, pointed to other secondary factors such as the shifting nature of the labour market in a sharing economy, the rise of entrepreneurism, the need for greater demographic inclusion, the shift towards higher education standards and the growth of the creative, knowledge and service economies in the future. [xiv]

The effect of all this will be massive. There are no guarantees with any job. Every job will be impacted to a more or lesser degree. Organisations will have a responsibility to upskill their staff. Staff will have to learn to adapt to change, be prepared to learn new skills and become learning agile.

People-focused roles will be the most valued in the future, for example, roles that are centred around collaboration, problem solving, creativity, innovation, critical thinking and analysis, and inductive thinking. Why? Because these skills will lie within roles that can't be automated or coded.

HUMILITY AND LEADERSHIP: HUMILITY IS THE LENS THROUGH WHICH YOU SHOW YOU CARE.

HBR's article (Chamorro-Premuzic, et al., 2018) on how AI will impact leadership moving forward, tells us that the soft skill of humility will be a critical leadership quality in the future.

Why is humility in leadership getting more and more attention?

As our business landscape continues to change exponentially, one thing will never change—us. People are complex and diverse. We're driven and motivated by different things.

Humble leaders see the potential and value in others because they are self-aware enough to value it without comparison to themselves. Being humble is appreciating that, at some level, we're all the same.

Being humble means appreciating that everyone has a life story and a contribution to make. Humble leaders appreciate that real thoughts and feelings are messy. They understand there is much more to someone than meets the eye. Leading with humility means finding the potential in others, rather than judging their development gaps.

When I interviewed John Chambers, it was apparent to me that he chose humility as his core leadership lens:

> Many people see leadership in the beginning as getting ahead or getting promoted. I see leadership, as having people follow what I put out there, so I can help them find out who they really are. People are the centre of how I think and do things. That doesn't mean I won't fire you if you're not up to the task. Ultimately, what I'm here for is to see you grow and for you to reach your full potential. I try to be humble every day. And the important thing is to be consistent so that people don't get surprised. It keeps me within my integrity.

THE NUMBER OF PEOPLE IN AN ORGANISATION DOESN'T MATTER. THE NUMBER OF PEOPLE WHO CAN THINK DOES.

The most essential skills when it comes to leading change are interpersonal skills, learning agility, and resilience. Underpinning all of this is being able to work with and through people to get things done. This depends on your ability to develop and leverage relationships.

People want to do their best work, and they are already motivated to do this. Why? Because we all share the same 'want' to make a meaningful contribution. People want to connect to their organisation, to feel like they're part of something bigger and to have a 'purpose' for being there that extends further than the job. I often ask my clients 'why does your career success matter and what will it give you?' There is a consistent theme to their answers: the opportunity to make a difference. We all want to make a positive contribution to others. However, the difference between leaders and followers is their focus. Leaders want to contribute to others so that results will be achieved. Followers want to contribute to results and they do this through others.

MAKING A DIFFERENCE HAPPENS
WHEN YOU CONNECT AND SHOW YOUR CARE
THROUGH WHO YOU ARE FOR OTHERS.

Leadership is about people. If you don't have people around you, there is no one to lead. Leadership is not about the strategy/planning, it's about people, communication and relationships. Everything else happens around these things. You do not lead things, you lead people. You have to care. If you don't care, you're not going to get anywhere. So you need to ask, how much do I care about people? You can't be a good leader without caring about people. You can be a good Manager but you'll never become a good leader. If you don't care about people, then you're on the wrong journey. Leadership is not about your self-esteem or ego. —*Carlos Shafer*

Making a difference to others is based on the degree to which you value relationships, and build trustful and meaningful connections. If you think about the best relationships you have at work and what makes them so successful, chances are, those relationships are based on trust, teamwork, communication and respect. Those are the four key elements to effective working relationships.

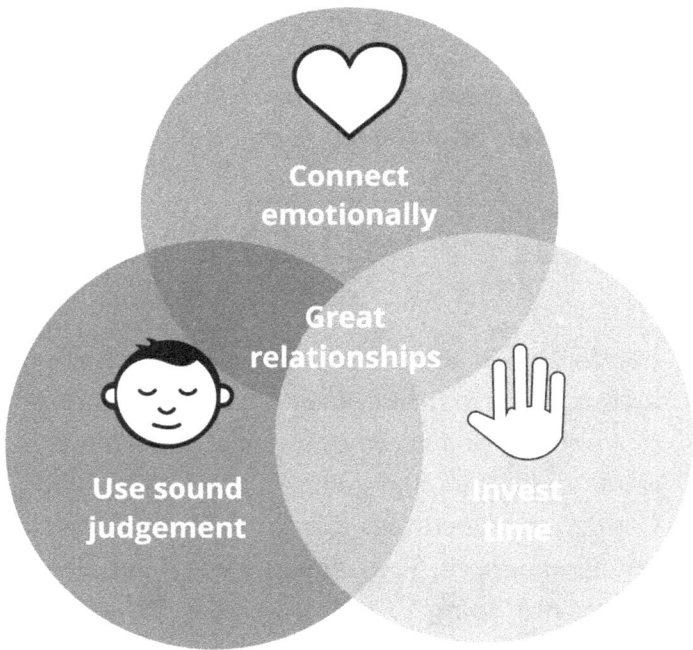

FIGURE 5: RELATIONSHIPS 'CARE' MODEL

MAKE IT REAL. MAKE IT PERSONAL. CONNECT EMOTIONALLY. **(YOUR HEART)**

As a leader, it's vital your team knows who you are, what's important to you, what drives you, and what success—for you and the team—looks like. Your team must 'get' you.

Every time I start with a new team, I give them the 'dummies guide to me'. I outline my family, my faith, my background, my kids—the things that really matter to me. This gives them a sense of who I am and how I like to work. It's exposed up front. So the first few meetings are about 10% on the current results and the rest is all about getting to know each other.

—John Chambers

There is much talk about harnessing diversity in teams. Diversity is deeper than gender, LGBT or other ways in which people are categorised. Diversity is a deep appreciation of who people are. It means developing bonds past the confines of someone's role and their daily activities. It means caring for the person they are as well as the contribution they make. It means seeing things from their perspective, from their belief system or value set.

EVERY RELATIONSHIP CAN TEACH US SOMETHING.

Many people hold the belief that people come into their lives for a reason—that there is no 'by coincidence' meeting.

A friend and mentor, John Fitzgerald, runs Custodian Wealthbuilders, a wealth education and property development company. At the age of 17, he backpacked to Brisbane with $200 in pocket, and by the age of 25, he owned $1 million in net property assets. He started out door knocking to get listings. At first, he hated it and then he learned to love it. His advice was to learn to love what you don't like doing. That piece of advice has stayed with me. We don't like doing things that take us out of our comfort zone, the things that are hard where we, for example, might be rejected or might not get the result we want. But by persisting we grow skills and capabilities that can impact every area of our lives. For John, all those hours door knocking gave him important knowledge and insights into how to build rapport, relationships and trust through listening to and working with others. Years later, I took John's advice to another level, and I learned to like (and even love) the people I didn't like.

While working at ANZ, I was faced with a peer who was condescending, rude, arrogant and helped others only when it made him look good. He knew his stuff and was politically savvy. His results were valued by our boss because, in my opinion, he made our boss look good. His attitude and behaviour were tolerated and frequently commented on. After a run-in with him, where he refused to help generate some customer reporting, I decided to step away from trying to engage with him further. Just after that incident, I heard that his marriage had broken down. I felt sorry for him. I knew what that was like. I reached out and offered my help and support. He appreciated having someone impartial with whom to talk. I saw a different side to him. I chose to like the sides of him I saw, and I'm glad I gave myself the opportunity to see those sides.

The key point here is that just because you don't like some sides of someone's personality doesn't mean you should write them off completely. After all, your perceptions of someone could be vastly different from someone else's. For example, behaviour that is arrogant to one person might be perceived as confident by another. Your ability to work with others from a place that is judgement-free means you can accept and value the contribution of others, appreciating that there are some sides of their behaviour that aren't in line with your values or expectations of how someone should have acted in a given circumstance. It's easy to assume a problem or gap lies with someone else; it's far less easy to spot the gap within ourselves. I've often heard leaders complain where a direct report has fallen short of expectation. They perceive they have been clear in their expectations because they've observed their report listening actively to them. Therein lies the problem. What they've communicated and what someone has understood the expectation to be is different. Communication effectiveness lies with the receiver not the communicator. Misaligned expectations are at the root of many relationship issues that become exacerbated by ego on both sides, where someone decides I can't work with this person. The question to ask ourselves is how can I work with this person? How do I need to show up?

INVESTING TIME IN RELATIONSHIPS ACCELERATES WHAT CAN BE ACHIEVED **(YOUR HANDS).**

It's convenient to think there will be time for relationships after the results are achieved. This thinking is a trap. Relationships require time, energy and conscious effort. Relationship building means prioritising time, for example, spending time with someone face-to-face rather than sending an email or ensuring you are well prepared to best leverage the value of one on one time with your boss.

MANAGING UP.

If your personal brand is your perceived business worth, then your ability to 'manage up' is critical. The most important relationship you have is with your boss. Managing upwards is a function of the spheres of influence you have. The more you are perceived to be accomplished, capable, and trustworthy, the higher degree of influence you'll have.

Mary was a high achiever and her team loved her. To them, she was a confident and empowering leader. However, Mary felt disconnected with her new boss Michael. Although he gave her lots of freedom, she felt undermined and worried when they couldn't align on the big-ticket projects. Things had to change. But how? Although Mary had been on board in her role for three months, she appreciated that she hadn't aligned with her boss on what was important to him. She hadn't taken the time to get a helicopter view on her boss's perspective of the business to understand, from his point of view, what they needed to accomplish, and what success looked like to him.

You may not agree with your boss on everything and why should you? Assuming there is a good level of trust, always remember to acknowledge their point of view. It's not a good idea for your boss to perceive that they're being made wrong on a judgement call. Remember your common ground. Beware of the language you use and ensure it's not confrontational. For example, 'I'm curious about whether we could ...' A good influencing tactic is to gain support for your ideas beforehand so it's not just coming from you. And, if a conversation becomes difficult, listen more than you talk. Chapter 7 has other influencing tactics to add to your toolkit.

INFLUENCE IS A JUDGEMENT GAME
(YOUR HEAD).

The game of influence isn't easy. Things are rarely black and white. There is often no clear path. Sound judgement is required at every part of the journey. You need to decide whether to hold off and wait or fight the battle ahead, all the while evaluating the different options to get ahead.

Patience is an underrated and critical virtue in leadership. Sometimes things need time. Maybe what you're focused on can't be looked at or achieved within your timeframe but maybe it's in someone else's timeframe. This is a difficult lesson for young leaders to learn. Things are sometimes in a different time zone than what you want. Sometimes it's hard letting go of the thing you want to progress. Appreciate that you may not have as full a picture as someone else.

There are other times, however, when doing a good job means pushing the envelope on something or ruffling a few feathers to challenge the status quo thinking, decision or action.

If you can't deal with confict, then don't get on the court. If you don't care or if you are more interested in protecting your job than doing a good job, you won't take a risk—that's not leadership.

—Carlos Schafer

THE ONLY THING YOU ARE IN CONTROL OF IS YOU. WHILE THIS MAY SOUND OBVIOUS—IT'S NOT.

Our need for control disconnects us in relationships.

We all know control freaks. They attempt to control the situation by controlling others or controlling how things need to be. Let's face it, we all love the feeling of being in control. We all get wedded to our opinion from time to time. Control meets our need for certainty.

I know someone who plans their family meals a week in advance, puts her t-shirts away in her drawers by colour, and schedules every activity by different colour codes on a calendar in the kitchen. I've also recently worked with a team whose reporting leader (let's call him Jim) is masterful at reframing what is said so he can take the lead in virtually every conversation. While reframing is a smart and powerful influencing tactic, Jim overuses it to take control, and in doing so, shuts down the conversation for others. This habit is impacting his team dynamic and performance. Although Jim wants his team to step-up more, he has taught them to be quiet around him while he provides the context and then the direction. Jim's need for control is making it easy for his team to follow his lead, but at the expense of their development. Jim can't have his cake and eat it too. Leadership and control don't work that way.

While creating a sense of control meets our own needs, needing to have control in a relationship will not nurture it in any way.

Do you like being in control more than you should? Here are some signs that the answer is yes:

- You believe others need to change in a way that aligns with your expectations of how they need to be.
- You want others to see and agree with your perspective first.
- You manage small details in a way that dictates how things need to be or look.
- You judge others' behaviour as good and bad, or right and wrong.

- When things don't go your way, you retreat (become passive aggressive) or retaliate. It's hard for you to let things go.
- You offer your constructive feedback/criticism based on your standards or expectations.
- You jump to conclusions easily.
- You point out when others are wrong, or you intervene between others.
- You struggle with ambiguity where things are 'up in the air'.
- You like to stick to the plan. You find it hard to cope when things could change, or when they do at the last minute.
- You care greatly about the impressions others have of you.
- You change how you normally show up to accommodate others, fit in and be liked. You'll be agreeable, change your story, or not voice an alternative view.
- You'll put others down in a way that makes you look good or be right.

Do any of these indicators resonate with you? Think about how they may be impacting your relationships in ways you may not realise. What if you gave up needing to have control? What would you need to give up specifically? How would your relationship change as a result?

As the leader, your standards—how you show up for others—sets the tone for how everything is done. It starts with you. Every decision you make, every action or non-action, tells others what you care about.

TRUST AND RAPPORT ENABLE EVERYTHING.

When you meet someone for the first time, you don't immediately have a relationship. These questions underpin the quality of your first interaction with someone: Do I like you? Do I want to work with you? Can I trust you? There are two critical pre-requisites to any relationship: rapport and trust.

The first step in having a relationship is building rapport. Do you notice how some people seem to develop rapport with others so effortlessly? They seem to know just what to say, how to say it, and when to say it in a way that enables people to warm to them quickly.

Rapport is the process of building a connection with someone based on shared understanding and commonality. It enables someone to feel comfortable, accepted and psychologically safe. There are many ways to build rapport with someone including asking open ended questions, active listening, matching and mirroring someone else's body language, tone, style or pitch, and acknowledging someone.

Deep listening is more than a valuable social habit; it is a transformative communication tool. With deep listening, you are not only allowing yourself the time and space to fully absorb what your conversation partner is saying, you can actually encourage him or her to feel heard and to speak more openly and honestly. And this is a key step in developing rapport with someone.

—Tony Robbins

Next comes trust. Trust has a lot to do with influence—both are earned. Once trust is gone, influence is an upward battle.

IT'S WHAT WE DO, NOT WHAT WE SAY, THAT DRIVES TRUST AND RESPECT IN RELATIONSHIPS.

You can't pick and choose who you work with and you probably have to work with people you don't like very much. Trust though, is always a personal choice. No one can make you trust them and vice versa. We have a trust bank in every relationship that is either building or eroding. Trust develops in a relationship when each party becomes trustworthy. Subtly, good leaders are able to earn the trust of others quickly. What you say, how you say it and how you follow through on the commitments you make are small but key indicators that people accumulate as they form their perceptions about you.

Building trust is also about having integrity—walking your talk, being congruent and having the courage to act in accordance with your values and beliefs.

THERE IS A MASSIVE TRUST GAP IN AUSTRALIAN BUSINESS.

I don't know if there's ever been a time when trust in our society was so low. Think about the instability and lack of trust in Australian politics, media, and sports to name a few. It's clear that trust is also at an all-time low across the business landscape. It might surprise you that only 38% of Australian leaders are rated as trustworthy (Swinburne Leadership Institute). Why is this?

The reality is that many organisations operate in silos, with short-term financial goals, low appetite for risk, and incremental predictable growth and returns. Managers rise through the ranks where predictability and control are rewarded, not disruption and innovation. Organisations operate with ingrained processes where how things are done is outdated and inefficient. They reflect the need for control and effectively breed scepticism and a lack of trust between levels of management. In an environment of distrust, people will work hard to protect their turf.

Oftentimes, underpinning these operating models are internal cultures where people 'do their bit' to look good, get the job done, and move onto the next task. Transactional attitudes are fostered where 'work is work' and 'it's just the way it is'. People achieve despite the cultural environment that surrounds them. People stay in environments like this for a variety of reasons but they are not happy or fulfilled. People complain about issues relating to communication or relationships; however, the core issue is a systemic lack of trust that runs through the organisation. Most organisations have a trust issue. Lack of trust makes collaboration hard because silo thinking exacerbates why things are the way they are.

WE NEED TO FIX THE TRUST GAP.

Fixing the trust gap starts with everyone taking responsibility for who they need to be to live the values (of their organisation) and be an example for others. An organisation's values reflect what is cared about the most within the organisation. The trouble is many organisations have a considerable gap between the values (the ideal for what the culture should be) and behavioural norms (what actually drives the culture). Because no one 'owns' the culture, it is put in the 'too hard' basket, where bad behaviours are tolerated and settled for. This starts from the top down and costs everyone, especially the leaders who are judged for not walking their talk. I share with leaders that the standard they walk passed is the standard by which their leadership will be judged. An example of this is where a leader says they value creativity, but someone in their team believes their ideas won't go anywhere so they don't speak up.

Building a positive culture starts with everyone aligning on living the values that drive individual behaviour, as well as the expectations for how people/teams work together. People who don't fall into line, get the feedback, and if it's not acted upon, get moved on. The standards are non-negotiable. Teams with great culture wouldn't want to operate any other way. Trust starts when we become trustworthy.

My business and relationships are built on trust. I have a philosophy of I do it for them, and they do the same for me. People are my big thing whether they're external or internal within by business. I care about

trust and authenticity. I value me and others doing their best. Sometimes I have to let people go, but it's always done with dignity and respect. Living the values and leveraging the diversity in my team is how I've built my team.

—Julie Rynski

Building trust is important and people do this intuitively. When I ask my clients how they are proactively building trust within their teams and organisation, most of the time, there is silence. Sharon Pearson, CEO of The Coaching Institute came up with these ways to proactively lead by example to build trust banks across your own relationships:

- **Show others respect.** Acknowledge and appreciate different backgrounds, opinions, feelings, values and belief systems.
- **Have open communication.** Know how to have purposeful conversations that stay on purpose and on track. Keep other people informed and share information that others value and need. Be transparent. People would rather know the real status as opposed to the positive spin.
- **Develop shared purpose and goals.** Acknowledge that while everyone will have different aspirations and motivations, develop ecological outcomes that will benefit everyone.
- **Have confidence in others' abilities.** Know how to achieve shared goals, and how to leverage each other's knowledge and skills.

HOW YOU CHANNEL YOUR EMOTIONS WILL MAKE OR BREAK YOUR RELATIONSHIPS.

I'm choosing to talk about emotional intelligence (EQ) last for a good reason. Everything I've spoken about so far, in this chapter, relates to emotional EQ in some way. Building genuine relationships and bonds with others is a function of your EQ.

We're always reacting emotionally. We are not designed to have a thought and not react in some way—it's instinctual. We can't turn emotions off. Our emotions tell us what we care about the most. Managing emotion is a critical skill for leadership performance. The biggest driver of your performance is your EQ. It contributes more than 50% to your performance and is more important than experience, IQ, talent and potential. EQ is what ties your performance and potential together more than anything else.

Emotional intelligence is that 'something' in each of us that is an intangible. It relates to how we manage our emotions, ourselves and our relationships with others. It affects how we manage behaviour, navigate social complexities, and make decisions that achieve positive results. At the heart of emotional intelligence is self-awareness. People with high self-awareness are good at managing their emotional state, they can self-reflect, they are thoughtful, and they are comfortable with ambiguity and not having all the answers.

Anyone can become angry—that is easy.
But to be angry with the right person, to the right
degree, at the right time, for the right purpose,
and in the right way—this is not easy.

—*Aristotle*

BUILDING EQ ENABLES YOU TO BECOME A MORE INTENTIONAL AND AUTHENTIC LEADER.

A coach asked me to write two points for each interaction I was due to have in a particular week. I was to consider how I wanted the other person to feel after our transaction (what was my objective?) After the interaction, I was to consider if I met my aim? This was the self-reflection point.

Every day, as I drive to work, I think about my work schedule, and who I'm going to meet. Then, on my way home, I'll self-reflect about those interactions. It's made me much more aware of things that I don't naturally want to do, but I think I owe it to others around me to take the space and do it.

Self-reflection is what it takes to build self-awareness: who we are being for ourselves, who we are being for others and how we are creating the experience someone else has of us.

—*Kylie Bishop*

Dr Travis Bradberry is an expert on EQ. His research shows that 90% of top performers are also high in emotional intelligence. On the flip side, just 20% of bottom performers are high in emotional intelligence. You can be a top performer without emotional intelligence, but the chances are slim.[xv]

Although some people are naturally more emotionally intelligent than others, you can develop high emotional intelligence over time. In addition to self-awareness and empathy, developing EQ means developing social and communication skills.

- **Social skills:** This is being able to read cues and signs between the lines of communication. We can speak volumes through our body language without saying a word. Social skills also include the way you work with others, and how you handle conflict and difficult conversations.
- **Communication skills:** Most relationship fallouts happen through a breakdown in communication. Dealing with difficult people becomes easier with experience. Learning to deal with difficult people is about holding the space and ensuring respect where everyone's input can be heard and acknowledged. Holding the space takes patience and empathy, and it takes courage to speak out and lead in a conversation. When everyone knows the direction and that everyone's contribution matters, it's much easier getting alignment from others when things go wrong.

Using these EQ skills to adapt to different personalities, team dynamics and environments is further explored in Chapter 6.

CHAPTER 6:

ADAPT YOUR LEADERSHIP STYLE FOR DIFFERENT SITUATIONS

INFLUENCE IS YOUR ABILITY TO ADAPT YOUR LEADERSHIP, IN ANY SITUATION, TO BE EFFECTIVE AND BRING OUT THE BEST IN THE PEOPLE WITH WHOM YOU ARE WORKING.

So far, we've looked at the relationship you have with yourself and your relationships with others. Both are complex and form the foundation for how you work with and through others to achieve results. The complexity doesn't stop there. The next step acknowledges the level to which the complexity of our work environment affects our ability to influence.

Your ability to continuously learn and adapt will determine the extent to which you will thrive in today's business environment. An essential leadership attribute is the ability to remain open to new ways of thinking and to learn new skills continuously.

Korn Ferry found that companies with highly agile executives have 25% higher profit margins than their peer group. Individuals with high learning agility are promoted twice as fast as individuals with low learning agility. [xvi]

LEADERSHIP DOESN'T HAPPEN IN ENVIRONMENTS THAT ARE STATIC.

In nature, a species that is able to evolve and adapt within a changing environment gives itself the greatest chance to survive and thrive. The same applies in business where leaders lead in a VUCA world. VUCA is an acronym created by the American Military to describe extreme conditions in which soldiers are required to work. It stands for Volatile, Uncertain, Complex and Ambiguous. Businesses that aren't prepared to change and adapt in these same conditions will lose the right to survive. Kodak is a well-known classic case that demonstrates how the fixed mentality of this is the way we do it, led to the company's demise. A more recent example is Blockbuster Video. Do you remember renting their movies or games years ago? At its peak, Blockbuster was one of the most recognised brands in the video rental space. Unable to transition towards a digital model, Blockbuster filed for bankruptcy in 2010. Interestingly, to add insult to injury, in 2000 Netflix approached Blockbuster with an offer to sell their company to Blockbuster for US$50 million. The Blockbuster CEO turned the offer down believing Netflix was a small niche business. As of July 2018, Netflix had over 130 million subscribers worldwide and is currently on schedule to produce over 80 original movies this same year— more than Disney.

In complete contrast, Apple—the most profitable and most respected business in the world and currently worth over $1 trillion—stays ahead of its competitors. It designs what people want, and it makes it better than anyone. Its attitude is to challenge the status quo: to do it different, to do it better. Apple's rise to the top reflects its remarkable agility. No other company comes close to Apple's ability to conquer new markets, one after another.

MANAGING PEOPLE IS FINE UNTIL LEADERSHIP IS REQUIRED.

Managers operate best in stable and process-driven environments where there is incremental predictable growth. In the past, command and control leaders were safe within these types of environments where this is the way we do it wasn't questioned.

In a VUCA world, the old command and control leadership style is no longer tolerated. In the last few years, I've witnessed aging command and control leaders, who were viewed as 'waiting to retire', be exited out into early retirement. Their removal from the organisation came as both a shock and a sense of relief signalling an anticipated change in organisational dynamics and culture.

No matter how certain or strong you are, or how well things worked before, as your surroundings change, you'll need to adapt to survive.

Indecision is changing one's mind without any new information. Adaption is changing one's mind in response to new information. Indecision slows you down, but adaption moves you forward.

—Doe Zantamata

So how can we be successful in a changing environment? The answer is by becoming behaviourally flexible.

GREAT MINDS DON'T THINK ALIKE.

In the future, successful leaders will be those who truly connect with others in a way that engages, influences and inspires. To do this, leaders need strong interpersonal skills. Without these, it will be an upward battle to bring others along and work in cohesive teams.

Strong leaders value and harness the thinking diversity of their team, and they use diversity as a driving factor when recruiting their team. More diversity leads to better outcomes.

A 2015 McKinsey report on 366 public companies found those in the top quartile for ethnic and racial diversity in management were 35% more likely to have financial returns above their industry mean, and those in the top quartile for gender diversity were 15% more likely to have returns above the industry mean.[xvii]

Harnessing diversity, however, requires a consultative approach where positive debate and conflict are embraced as a way to challenge, stretch and shape people's thinking. Easy thinking isn't the benchmark. Great thinking challenges the status quo and explores new solutions to new problems. Leading diverse teams requires leadership that can adapt to the thinking styles of others and lead thinking from exploration through to decisions, actions and results. Capitalising on diversity means acknowledging, not hiding from, differences.

LEADERSHIP IS KNOWING THE RIGHT APPROACH FOR THAT SITUATION.

I share with my clients that they can't expect to be effective by responding to every situation in the same way. Think of this version of insanity: doing the same thing repeatedly and expecting a different result. If we only have a small number of ways of responding and reacting, they will often miss the mark, and that is where stress can arise on both sides causing misunderstanding, frustration, irritation and annoyance.

Behavioural flexibility is the ability to respond in different ways to different situations acknowledging that people think and see things differently. People are motivated by different things. Our emotional states are situational. Leadership occurs in shades of grey with ambiguity and complexity — there often isn't one 'right' view. That is, the decision is not binary and the 'right' decision still needs to be made. Every situation potentially has new or different context. Behavioural flexibility describes our ability to 'flex' our core behaviours so that we respond to each circumstance in the most effective way.

The person with the most flexibility of thought, for example, judgements and perceptions that create their feelings, communication and behaviour will have the edge over others who have less in their toolkit. In other words, the heart of behavioural flexibility is the belief that the person with the most flexibility is controlling the system—more choice is better than less choice. This presupposition comes from the *Law of Requisite Variety* and is a core Neuro Linguistic Programming principle.

Lack of behavioural flexibility explains why many leaders fail in new role transition. They are unable to adapt into a new work environment and culture. In fact, in the USA, approximately 40% of new executive hires fail in the first 90 days. The biggest derailer for new recruits is the inability to integrate into a new culture. In addition, lack of behavioural flexibility shows why C-Level leaders, who work best in fast paced, results centred environments, are unable to show enough understanding and empathy to lead organisations through effective change that sticks.

Average leaders come in with one or two hats. Great leaders have many hats – they can adapt to lots of different situations that require different things.

—Michael Ehrentraut

THE PERSON WHO IS THE MOST ADAPTABLE AND VERSATILE WILL HAVE THE MOST INFLUENCE.

Ultimately the person with the most influence is leading.

Marc was a Project Manager. His typical influencing approach was to convince others by backing his ideas with the facts, figures and rationale. There was a business case to support his initiative after all, so in his mind a data based influencing approach was a no brainer. So why were people not listening? When his ideas weren't supported, Marc came back with more data and rationale. Marc could see he needed more to win people over. He began to form closer ties with his key stakeholders, spent more time understanding their business, listened to their challenges and frustrations. He was then able to articulate the project benefits in a more compelling way, tweak the change process along the way and make the 'benefit' list in the business case even longer. He learned that when people are involved in the decision making and have a say in how things get done, their increased engagement and accountability will lead to even better outcomes.

When you adapt your style to others, it will help you build much better bridges to them.

HOW WOULD YOU DESCRIBE YOUR STYLE?

We all have a preferred or natural leadership style, which encompasses our preferred way of thinking, our drivers and dominant behaviours, how we typically engage with people, and how we prefer to work. If you think about running a successful project, you need the strategic big picture thinkers who can outline the goals and objectives and tell you why 'achieving' matters. You also need people who can prepare the plans, organise the resources and rally others together. You need the conscientious doers who love pulling their sleeves up and keeping their eye on the details. And, you also need the people who bring great ideas and energy, and thrive by working with others to keep everyone on track. Each skill set has a contribution to make and each contribution complements each other.

The greater the impact you want to make, the greater your influence needs to be. In order to reach your potential as a leader, you must understand your unique leadership style.

—*John Maxwell*

Understanding your predominant behaviours will go a long way towards helping you determine not only your preferred style but also why you operate that way.

- Are you more extroverted or introverted?
- Are you a big picture thinker or do you love the detail?
- Do you prefer to work from a plan or figure it out as you go along?
- Do you think before you speak or speak and think afterwards?
- Do you like to win (outcome focused) or are you more interested in enjoying the game (journey focused)?

The easiest way of knowing your style is to undergo a personality or behavioural profile, for example DiSC. This type of profiling will test your strengths and stretches against certain benchmarks or criteria used to classify people into different leadership styles.

OUR LEADERSHIP STYLE WILL DETERMINE OUR PREFERENCES FOR HOW WE ENGAGE AND INFLUENCE OTHERS.

In 2009 and 2010, Discovery Learning, Inc. and Innovative Pathways conducted research to identify and measure influence styles. They created five categories:

1. **Asserting**: you insist that your ideas are heard, and you challenge the ideas of others.
2. **Convincing**: you put forward your ideas and offer logical, rational reasons to convince others of your point of view.
3. **Negotiating**: you look for compromises and make concessions to reach outcomes that satisfy your greater interest.
4. **Bridging**: you build relationships and connect with others through listening understanding and building coalitions.
5. **Inspiring**: you advocate your position and encourage others with a sense of shared purpose and exciting possibilities.

Each of these styles can be effective, depending on the situation and people involved.

Of course, different styles will suit different people in different situations. The goal isn't to become equally strong in every style but to acknowledge and appreciate your own style and be able to step into other styles with enough skill needed when the situation calls for it.

PEOPLE DON'T WANT TO BE CONTROLLED, THEY WANT TO BE SHOWN HOW TO SUCCEED.

Every strength has a flipside. In a recent coaching session with Jess, I asked her about her natural leadership style. Core to her leadership style was leveraging her knowledge (having previously assumed the roles of her direct reports) to deliver results. She led from the front, knowing the detail, having the right answers, and ensuring her team output met her high standards. She felt her expectations were appropriate despite feeling her team was frequently falling short of meeting them, validating her belief that she needed to be over every bit of detail. She realised that while this approach met her own needs for certainty and control, she was letting her team down. She was a leader who simply, in a nice way, told others what to do. Wanting to be a nurturing leader, Jess saw the gap between her intention and impact. Being at the front and centre of everything was actually a disservice to her team. The 'flex' opportunity for Jess was to assess the opportunities of which to let go, to feel comfortable in conversations exploring the answers and options with her team, and encouraging her team to create the solution. The upside for Jess was teaching her team to think and take the initiative.

BEHAVIOURAL FLEXIBILITY INCREASES WHEN, OVER TIME, YOU DO SOMETHING DIFFERENT.

So, in practical terms, what does being behaviourally flexible mean? Simply, you have lots of choices when it comes to reacting and responding in any situation. For example, you can adapt how and when you communicate (what you say and how you say it), how you behave (what you do) and how you use your body (your physicality and body language).

You might choose to be more assertive and speak your mind, or step back and observe how others respond. You might choose to listen more actively or offer your opinion. You might say a strong 'no', or you might ask for advice. Rather than show frustration, you can choose to stay calm and be patient until you have more information. You might use humour to connect with a new group of people. You are more empathetic when you give critical feedback. You share the purpose for making a change before getting straight into the detail about what needs to change. Rather than judge someone, you ask questions to understand why they made that decision. Lastly, you might go with your gut feel rather than what the figures are telling you.

Think about your natural style and consider some ways you could flex this style to become even more effective.

THE DEGREE TO WHICH YOU CAN INFLUENCE, IS THE DEGREE TO WHICH YOU CAN BE INFLUENCED.

Let's take a deeper look into behavioural flexibility.

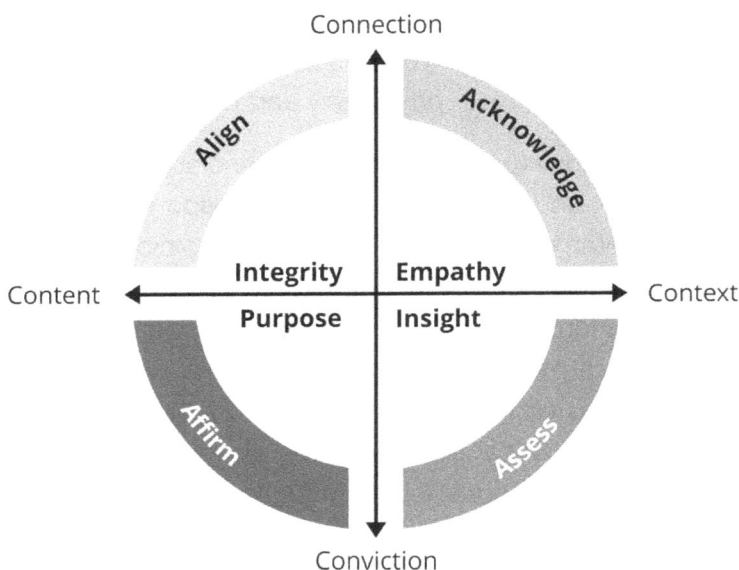

FIGURE 6: ADAPTIVE LEADERSHIP MODEL

My model is defined by four dimensions:

Conviction: what we know to be true from our knowledge bank of information, generalisations, biases, and assumptions.

Connection: the strength of relationships we have with others.

Content: an opportunity, need or purpose that brings people together and enables them to share in a common goal.

Context: the environment that people are operating within that defines how people work together to achieve a result.

There are four key building blocks for behavioural flexibility:

Assess. Be insightful. This highlights the opportunity to expand your thinking to discover and evaluate different perspectives to see, for example, what a win/win might look like. Doing this involves understanding and appreciating the complexity and ambiguity of what data exists and what data doesn't exist. It involves being able to shut up, listen, and be present, to understand what is being said, to read between the lines, spot the gaps and inconsistencies, and pick up on non-verbal cues that might exist in your or someone else's reasoning. It's about listening to find the greater good rather than to validate your own thinking; its about adding to your thinking in an inclusive way that enables you to lead forward and connect with others at the same time.

Your biggest asset is your ability to think and contribute that thinking in a way that adds value to others. Being non-judgemental and using sound judgement in decision-making is a skill and practice. When you listen first and speak later, your message adds value rather than opinion. You'll build influence.

Acknowledge. Be empathetic. This highlights the opportunity to appreciate how others are thinking and feeling. It involves being able to put yourself into someone else's shoes and consider what their thinking might be. It involves asking open ended questions to discover frames like: How could they be thinking about this? Why? What might their concerns be? What might they need? What is important to them? What might they want you to understand about them? How will you demonstrate you've understood where they are coming from? Then you can use this as a base to help determine your approach.

The more you appreciate someone else's world, what motivates them and what drives their decision-making, the more impactful you'll be. Start from their point of view, not your own. Find out their problems and solve them. This will earn you the right to speak, be heard and have influence.

Align: Have integrity. This highlights the need to be proactive and to meet the needs of others and the organisation in a way that aligns others and brings them together. It's about doing the right thing for a greater good. There will be times when people don't like the business decisions made. Having integrity means saying what needs to be said in a way that creates shared understanding, even if the decision made is not popular.

People don't have to like it, but if they can accept it and see the rationale, then it's their choice to move on or not.

Affirm: Be purposeful. This highlights the need to be decisive and to act with volition enabling agreements and reaching the next steps as the pathway forward. It's easy for people to say yes and do nothing or say yes and complain to others. Being purposeful ensures everyone knows what they have agreed to, what promises/commitments have been made, and the expectations for what happens next. In other words, people can agree and disagree on something initially, but when a decision is made, it's done on the basis there is an agreement to accept the decision and commitment to move forward in an aligned way. You can disagree before the decision is made, but you can't not commit after it's made. Teams who don't commit to shared goals and pathways are not effective.

WHY DOES BEHAVIOURAL FLEXIBILITY MATTER SO MUCH?

Simon Sinek said there's only one pre-requisite for leadership and that's to have followers. Leaders need their team with them or they're simply going for a walk on their own. It's a mistake to think that, as the leader, you have to be the front and centre of your team all the time. Having followers means bringing others with you. Bringing others with you happens when you can lead from the front, side and behind.

LEADERS NEED TO LEAD FROM THE FRONT, SIDE AND BEHIND.

Whoever is best to lead in that moment, for that situation, should do so. And if that's someone other than the leader, that's great.

A leader brings their team with them. They understand the need for their team to be beside them, in front of them and behind them, depending on where individual team members are in their own development journey.

In *The 360 Degree Leader,* John Maxwell says, 'Great leaders don't use people so they can win. They lead people so they can all lead together. If that is truly your motivation, you can become the kind of person that people want to follow – whether they are beside, above, or below you in the organisational hierarchy'.

LEADING FROM THE FRONT:

Leaders must be able to set the direction and pace based on their vision for what success is for the team, and stay on course through the inevitable challenges and setbacks. Leaders also need to focus on the key priorities that will win the game, and remove the obstacles that will hinder their team's progress. Leading from the front means walking your talk and living your values and principles consistently. To have influence, leaders need to set the example and be the example—without compromise, every day.

LEADING FROM THE SIDE:

Leaders must know how to be part of their team and contribute to ideas and solutions. Collaboration comes from harnessing individual strengths where there is no one right answer. Collaboration allows you to see your strengths, stretches and gaps in your own thinking. No leader has all the right answers all of the time. A leader also needs to contribute and add value across their peer network identifying opportunities and tackling issues in a collaborative way. It's easy to forget that we're contributing to various teams at any one time. Neglecting to see we have a responsibility to co-lead across our peer level collaboratively is a common mistake leaders make when they are too focused on their own team's delivery.

LEADING FROM BEHIND:

One of the hardest leadership lessons of all is giving up ownership (and a perceived sense of control) to let others lead. This doesn't mean giving other people your ideas, it means taking a step back, and letting others make the decisions, take the risks, and own the consequences. As a leader, knowing what someone is ready for, and inviting them into opportunities to step up and take the lead is one of the ways to accelerate someone's learning and development.

I've completed the personal development program The Landmark Forum. In the last part of the curriculum, the Self-expression and Leadership Program, every participant had to create a project that would make a significant positive difference to others. Everyone was fired up and enthusiastic about their projects. We had to pull a plan together and present it to the group. My idea was to bring all of the marketing folk in Westpac (my employer at the time) together for a one-day event to share info, ideas, insight and best practice, and to celebrate, as a community, what was being achieved. Fortunately, my idea was well received and supported by the senior leaders. For everyone on the program, the next instruction came as a surprise. We were told to assign our projects to another leader who would lead our projects to fruition. You can imagine the response. Some rebelled by ignoring the request; they could not bear to give up their projects. Others responded by worrying about how it would affect them personally. Others responded with curiosity about what was to come. No one found it easy and no one told us the rationale behind what we'd been asked to do. We all had a choice to make. It didn't occur to me, until years later, what an important leadership lesson it was. Leadership is never about you, it's about creating opportunities for others to shine. Self-involved leaders who resist giving up control— consciously or unconsciously— make it hard for everyone else around them to succeed.

LEADERSHIP OCCURS IN SHADES OF GREY.

There is no 'right' leadership style, behaviour or benchmark. If 'perfect' existed (instead of being in the mind's eye of the beholder), then it must exist in balance. Like, for example, the balance of our eco-system that provides the ideal conditions for a species to thrive, or the balance in our diet that allows us to enjoy whatever we like to eat while being healthy, or the balance of flavours that make a perfect meal. Leadership is the same. There is no universal trait that makes the perfect leader. The secret is to understand the flip side of your strengths and be self-aware enough to adapt as necessary to be effective.

LEADERSHIP IS PERCEPTION.

Just because you think you're displaying a particular leadership competency, if no one else it seeing or experiencing it, then to them, you don't have it. This fact is a big pill for some leaders to swallow. How you show up for others is their perception of you; it's not the truth, but it is their truth. That's why getting useful feedback is so important. Getting useful feedback from your boss, peers and team goes beyond how well you met the goals or the deadlines. It uncovers how your colleagues feel about working with you, how well you communicate and collaborate with them, and how you handle stress and adversity.

BEHAVIOURAL FLEXIBILITY IS SOMETHING YOU CAN DEVELOP OVER TIME THROUGH PRACTICE, EXPERIENCE, AND LEARNING FROM YOUR EXPERIENCES.

To become more adaptive, you must be prepared to try new behaviours and be open to feedback. You must expect that sometimes your new behaviour will result in the outcome you want, while other times it won't. Through the process, you'll learn something about yourself and others. Increasing your behavioural repertoire takes time and effort. Getting out of your comfort zone might be challenging, but the positive impact on your results has to be worth it.

BEING BEHAVIOURALLY FLEXIBLE IS MORE THAN THE BEHAVIOUR; IT COMES FROM TAKING ON NEW BELIEFS AND VALUES, AND CHALLENGING OUR ASSUMPTIONS.

Sarah wanted to become more assertive with her boss. Her boss had also given her the feedback she needed to be more assertive in meetings. During our chat, Sarah recalled a time as a child when she asserted herself with her older sister to get what she wanted. Her older sister reacted by walking away. Sarah felt deeply hurt and rejected. To her, it was clear that assertiveness and rejection went hand in hand. As a consequence of that decision, Sarah avoided situations involving conflict, preferring instead to go with the flow and keeping quiet. In the workplace, Sarah's strategy to feel safe enough to speak up in meetings was to ensure she had the facts to back up her opinion. For Sarah, being right minimised her risk of being rejected. In order for Sarah to 'flex' and become more assertive, she needed to believe that her views and opinions were of value, that her opinions weren't right or wrong, they were simply opinions. With this belief, Sarah could see the opportunity to say what she wanted without fear of being judged and rejected. Her leadership voice grew and so did her influence.

YOUR EMOTIONAL INTELLIGENCE (EQ) SITS BETWEEN YOUR THINKING AND YOUR BEHAVIOUR.

We experience our world through emotion. Managing our emotions and ourselves isn't easy. We make most of our decisions based on emotion, not logic. Emotion can be useful; therefore, it's not about shutting emotion down but channeling emotion effectively and not letting it get in the way of how we want to show up for ourselves and others.

While your IQ is fixed, your EQ is not—it's a learned skill every leader requires in today's business environment. You can't have a successful career and not have EQ. In fact, the leaders I rate most highly, lead through an EQ lens.

The best leaders are aware of the stories they tell themselves about how things are. Viktor Frankl was an Austrian psychiatrist as well as a Holocaust survivor. He pointed out the space between a stimulus (something happening) and our response, where he believed we had the freedom to choose our response.

This distinction is now known as Emotional Agility, which was coined by Susan David, a Harvard psychologist. Emotional agility means having difficult or challenging thoughts and emotions, and still managing to act in a way that serves you. In other words, not letting your emotion get the better of you.

Ultimately, how you respond and what you choose to take responsibility for will make or break what you can achieve. Being able to separate out what happened vs what you made it mean, so you can choose a different perspective that will serve you better.

YOU CAN'T CHANGE WHAT HAPPENED BUT YOU CAN CHOOSE HOW YOU FEEL ABOUT IT.

Would you like to change some of your stories and how you feel about them? My advice is to follow these three steps:

1. **Recognise:** Be curious about the stories you tell yourself. Chances are, they'll be more than you think when you start to notice them.

   George hasn't been back in touch and didn't respond to my last email. I must have disappointed him in some way when we last spoke. I wonder what I've done wrong, and I'm feeling a bit anxious.

2. **Reframe:** Choose another meaning by using a different perspective. Ask yourself how you could I think about this in a more objective or resourceful way.

   George has a number of important projects running to tight deadlines; he's under the pump. This is a really busy time. I feel for him and the pressure he's under.

3. **Resolve:** Decide what you're going to do (doing something or nothing is still a decision).

   I'm going to call George and offer to lend him a hand with his projects. Even if he says no, asking him is the right thing to do, and I feel good about that.

We can't feel anything without creating the thinking that drives the feeling. People can't make us feel anything; we always get to choose. In the example above, choosing a different perspective enabled the associated feeling to change from anxious to good.

The more emotionally aware we are the more behaviourally flexible and 'others focused' we can become. How others experience our ability to adapt to different personalities, situations and environments is through our leadership voice.

CHAPTER 7

BUILD INFLUENCE THROUGH YOUR LEADERSHIP VOICE

YOUR LEADERSHIP IS MORE ABOUT WHO YOU 'ARE' THAN WHAT YOU 'DO'.

IQ and competence will only get you so far. There's a certain point in any career where incremental gains in competence provide a diminishing return on performance. At this point, leaders need to focus on building influence through their leadership voice. Confident intentional leaders have a commonality: their sense of self matches who they are for those around them. In other words, you need to develop your leadership voice from the inside out.

**You are in integrity when the life you are living
on the outside matches who you are on the inside.**

—Alan Cohen

Influence is more than learning influencing tactics. The road to influence, once you learn strategies for confidence, know how to develop strong relationships, and how to adapt your natural style (all these pre-requisites for influence are covered in previous chapters), is about developing your leadership voice, so that your influencing tactics will be effective. The sequence is important. There is no silver bullet or shortcut. Your voice is a powerful leadership tool that influences people's perception, drives communication and helps you articulate your vision. A strong leadership voice will ensure you are heard, valued and recognised. The stronger your leadership voice, the more influence you will have.

WHAT IS YOUR LEADERSHIP VOICE?

Having a strong leadership voice means trying different communication approaches to managing people and getting decisions made.

Although we all have a voice, many leaders acknowledge their leadership voice is far quieter than they would like. Often, leaders work in environments where the loudest voices reign over others, where the consensus rules, and where (I hate to say it) the boys club pulls rank. These cultural and behavioural norms minimise quieter voices in decision-making, collaboration and problem solving. In these types of environments, leaders without a strong leadership voice feel shut down or shut out and don't take responsibility for having the voice they desire.

They:

- don't voice their views and ideas freely
- don't give the feedback and have the tough conversations
- follow the decisions of others instead of doing what they really want to do
- second guess actions or steps they take
- remain with the status quo or don't take enough action.

Your leadership voice has nothing to do with how loud you are. A great leader and influencer isn't necessarily the extrovert in the room. It's about speaking with persuasive power for a good purpose: leading the way you want to make a positive difference to others.

Building your influence, voice and brand relies on you stepping into spaces to create, drive, own, and deliver change that matters, rather than simply contributing to it as part of a team. A great question to ask yourself is: What am I causing? What change am I leading? And eventually: what did I deliver?

THE BIGGEST ENEMY TO YOUR LEADERSHIP VOICE IS HIDING BEHIND OTHERS.

Developing your leadership voice is not about trying to be like someone else. Your leadership starts with defining who you are as a leader—your leadership identity. It's about bringing your values into your leadership, being true to your principles and walking your talk without compromise. It's about having the capacity to back yourself and feel comfortable enough to 'do the thing' in spaces where there is uncertainty, fear and self-doubt.

Your leadership voice is heard in many ways beyond what you say. It is mirrored through the strengths of your own style, how you walk your talk, the energy you bring and your overall presence. Think about how you communicate. How do you solve problems, handle conflict, encourage collaboration, deliver feedback, and celebrate success? Your answers to these are your leadership voice.

Feedback can help you understand if your presence is working so you can align your verbal and non-verbal communication with the presence you want to have, and flex from your natural style.

Integrating your leadership identity, style and voice is an ongoing process of reflection and feedback.

Your intentional and authentic leadership voice is how you bring all facets of your leadership together in a way that's true to you. The model below demonstrates how each facet of your leadership is intrinsically connected to create your leadership brand. To be a leader with influence and impact, each facet of your leadership needs to complement and support the other.

Don't let the noise of others' opinions drown out your own inner voice.

—Steve Jobs

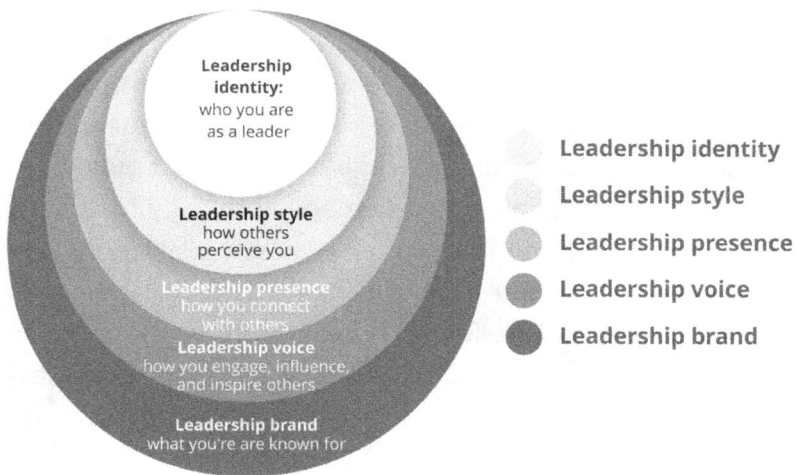

Leadership identity:
who you are as a leader

Leadership style
how others perceive you

Leadership presence
how you connect with others

Leadership voice
how you engage, influence, and inspire others

Leadership brand
what you're are known for

- Leadership identity
- Leadership style
- Leadership presence
- Leadership voice
- Leadership brand

FIGURE 7: FACETS OF YOUR LEADERSHIP

YOUR LEADERSHIP VOICE IS EITHER WORKING FOR YOU OR AGAINST YOU.

Tina was a well-regarded Senior Manager whose team loved her wit and confidence. In more senior leadership forums though, she remained quiet instead of speaking up, which meant she had to follow someone else's decision instead of doing what she really wanted. Tina let the chatter in her head get the better of her.

She judged herself negatively for letting herself down. The times when she did speak, she spoke tentatively, concerned about how her input was being heard (and judged). Tina realised that keeping quiet was affecting her contribution and she didn't have the influence she needed to build her brand. The starting point for Tina was to trust her opinion or view (which was really about Tina trusting herself and valuing her own contribution). She forced herself, even when her heart was racing, to have a voice and speak her mind, especially when her view when against the conversation flow. Over time, she developed new reference points to validate why she could own her leadership voice. In meetings, others began to look in her direction for input and this fuelled her desire to build proactively her communication toolkit, so she would be heard.

HBR's article *You Don't Just Need One Leadership Voice — You Need Many* suggested leaders cultivate enough parts of their voice, so that regardless of the situation or audience they face, they can respond in a way that's authentic and constructive. Here's my interpretation of the article's five voices. Each one will give a different experience of your leadership.

1. Your voice of character

This part of your voice is about you being constant and consistent. Your character matters more than your results. Your team need to recognise what you value and what you care about. This is how you lead from the inside out, in a way though, that's not 'all about you'.

As a leader, you want to stand for something. But not so much, that there's no room for anyone else to stand for something too. Your values don't make you right. They are not a crux. That's ego. There's no humility in that.

—Kylie Bishop

2. Your voice of context

Leadership and influence are perception and context based. Navigating the shades of grey and not losing sight of the bigger picture is important. Others are looking for certainty from you. When we're under pressure, it's easy to cut to the chase, give the direction, and step away. We believe telling our expectations is enough. Context gives meaning that enables peoples to understand, appreciate and accept what the expectations or decisions are, even if they're not agreed with.

If you don't share the context, people will make it up and probably get it wrong.

3. Your voice of clarity

We're all busy with multiple demands on our time. Saying 'yes' to the work that matters and 'no' to great ideas will keep you on track. Stay on your game and don't get distracted by shinny things.

Remind the team why they're there, what they're doing and why it matters. People want to know what success with you is like. Some will care about the end game, others will care more about the focus this week. Give others the clarity the need.

4. Your voice of curiosity

No one thinks exactly as you do. When you think differently, your experience of something will change. Are you asking enough questions? How often do you challenge your status quo? Do you push passed the easy thinking into spaces that hold new insight, ideas and solutions?

> **You can't solve problems with the same thinking that created them.**
>
> —*Albert Einstein*

5. Your voice of connection

Your voice of connection is reflected in how you share stories, acknowledge others, get to know others, show vulnerability, and share your vision. When people connect emotionally, they care and commit more. Take time to find out what motivates people and weave this into your communication—people will listen.

Remember to lead from your heart as well as your head.

WHAT IS THE LEADERSHIP VOICE YOU WANT TO OWN?

I want to ask you again: who is the leader you want to become in the next 2–5 years? What leadership voice do you need to develop to become that version of a leader?

Finding your voice, as a leader, comes from a belief in your ability to contribute and add value to others—to not hold back. Finding your voice also comes from using your voice consciously. Studies show we want two things from speakers: credibility and trust. Credibility is all about how you communicate. Do you speak quietly, too fast or too slow (or too much)? How do you phrase your sentences? When you listen to leaders whom you admire and respect, how do they project their voice and show their self-assuredness? Do you notice the tone of their voices and the attitude reflected in what they say and how they say it?

WHAT DOES IT MEAN TO BE A LEADER WITH A STRONG LEADERSHIP VOICE?

Your leadership voice is not fixed; it will evolve over time as you gain experience, and exposure to working with and leading different personalities, group dynamics, and cultural environments.

FIGURE 8: LEADERSHIP VOICE MODEL

Here are the key dimensions to your leadership voice that builds credibility and trust:

Courage (how you feel)

If you really want to do something, you'll find a way. Otherwise, you'll find an excuse.

Courage and confidence (as discussed in Chapter 4) happen in action. It's only in the 'doing' that we become the person we want to be. We can't read a book about courage and expect we'll have courage. Courage is a muscle that we build over time by facing fear and getting into action. Fear can stand in our way or not. The difference is how we manage fear, so we don't let it stop us or hold us back. Only in the face of fear, can courage show up. If you want a different result, you have to be prepared to do something different.

Conviction (what you know)

Your leadership voice is reflected in how you bring others with you. If your team doesn't believe you when you speak, it's unlikely to lean in when you need it to.

Have trust in what you know. You're not expected to know everything, have all the answers, and have polished and completed thinking all the time. Trust that you know enough to have a go and do your best. Backing yourself is a decision to believe that others will value your contribution; it starts by you deciding to value you and your contribution first. If you don't believe in you, why should others? When you speak with conviction, others can connect with you and 'get you'.

Clarity (what you communicate)

Powerful communication is about 'giving' rather than 'getting' and ensuring your messages are tailored to the needs of your audience.

Use your voice consciously. Be purposeful by speaking into someone else's listening and engaging them from their thinking set (their views, perspectives, ideas and opinions) rather than assuming they will automatically be influenced by you speaking from your thinking set. Speak slowly, breath deliberately, and deliver your messages clearly. To do that, you're going to have to think about how you pitch your message and how you 'chunk' information so that your audience can connect the levels in your logic and be clear about your communication. The benchmark of effective communication is what the listener has heard and understood, not what the speaker has said.

It's also not just what you say but also how you say it. Watch the confident leaders around you. Look at how their body looks when they address others. Usually, they are relaxed with open body language.

Keep your message simple enough to be understood, interesting enough to be remembered, and, most importantly, respectful enough of others to be respected.

—Joel Garfinkle

BRING YOUR LEADERSHIP VOICE TO LIFE.

The more influencing tactics you've got in your toolkit, the more influence you will have.

I mentioned upfront in this book that influencing is more than a list of influencing tactics to learn; however, I appreciate building a breadth of them will enable your leadership voice to be heard in any situation.

Below is a list of proven common influencing tactics that are incredibly impactful when used well. Have a think about which ones you're already using, and which ones you can begin to use with volition.

When you bring your whole and best self, and serve others first, you've earned the right to own your leadership voice. The next stage in your development journey is to take charge and develop your leadership voice so you can be heard and have the influence and impact you want.

INFLUENCING TACTIC	EXAMPLE
The power of **reciprocity:** Give first. *When you give to others first, they have a predisposition to want to give back to you.*	*I'm so appreciative of the help you've just given me. Now I need to reach out and ask you for a favour.*
Reframe: Help create a different way of looking at a situation, person, or relationship by changing its meaning. *When you change the way someone sees or experiences something, their perceptions can change dramatically.*	*You might think he is stingy with money, but that same attitude to money has enabled him to put his children through private schools.*
Ask great **questions:** *Asking great questions invites someone to step into new/different thinking spaces they create for themselves. High quality questions can influence someone very quickly.*	*Here are some general coaching questions that can work well in any conversation:* *What is the result you're looking to achieve here? (Why does that matter?)* *What's happening now? (How is this a problem for you?)* *What have you tried so far? (What is missing/getting in the way/holding you back?)* *How have you handled something like this before? (What was the outcome?)* *How else could you approach this? (What ideas do you have? What else can also be possible/true?)* *What's the first thing you're going to do to resolve/achieve this? (Eg: What would that conversation sound like when you talk with ...?)*

INFLUENCING TACTIC	EXAMPLE
	What resources do you need? (Does anyone else need to be involved? How else can I support you around your efforts to complete this?)
	What are you willing to commit to doing/trying/changing (by when)? (If you couldn't use that excuse/thing that's stopping you anymore, how would you move forward?)
	When would it make sense for us to reconnect to ensure you have achieved the result you want?
	I'm so appreciative of the help you've just given me. Now I need to reach out and ask you for a favour.
Understand the **motivations of others:** What do they care about, for example, are they motivated by doing the right thing, by status or recognition, or by learning new skills? *We're all motivated by different things. When you tap into someone's internal motivation currency, you can tailor your communication accordingly. Understanding what motivates someone comes from listening to them.*	For example, someone who is motivated by status: *This project is a high-profile project on our CEO's priority list. The benefits of this project will directly impact our customer satisfaction scores, which is why you'll have the opportunity to work directly with the Executive Team.*

INFLUENCING TACTIC	EXAMPLE
Use **social proof:** *We are social creatures. We rely heavily on other people around us for cues on how to think, feel and act. Persuasion can be extremely effective when it comes from peers. This tactic comes from Robert B. Cialdini, an expert on influence.*	In the below scenario, you would ask your direct report, Sam, to share his insight and learnings to influence the rest of the team to come on board. *I appreciate you're finding this new system a bit tricky, so I want to ask our team member Sam, who has gotten himself up to speed with it, to talk to us about how he's been able to transition so quickly to the new system and the difference it's made to his workload.*
Know how to **handle objections** in advance: *A smart way to handle anticipated objections is to be upfront and address them early on in your conversation.*	*If you're already wondering about the budget and where it's going to come from, what we've done is... so, now let's return to why this project....* **Common objections:** • No interest (you solve this by accurately expressing the urgency of the problem). • No perceived difference (you have your unique difference ready to go). • No belief (offer unquestionable proof that this works). • No decision (make their decision as user-friendly as possible).

INFLUENCING TACTIC	EXAMPLE
Create urgency: *Establish clearly why this important now and for what purpose. Bring the benefits/negatives into now.*	*By delaying this decision another month, we'll incur additional costs of $X, which we haven't budgeted for. To not incur those costs and deliver this budget on time, we need to make this decision today.*
Come back to the **common ground:** *When the conversation or negotiation gets challenging, come back to what everyone has agreed to, and lead the conversation from there.*	*It's clear there are some differing views here, and I want to remind everyone that our goal is to achieve the best customer experience, so let's reset on the criteria we've agreed to make this decision and go around the table again for your input.*
Lead the **chunk level** in the conversation: *The person controlling the chunk level is leading. A chunk level is a level of specificity in a conversation. Develop your ability to chunk up, across and down.*	• Chunk up: *For what purpose is that important to you? Let's look at the bigger picture here.* • Chunk across: *What's another idea? Or, what's another example of that?* • Chunk down: *What's the next step to take here? Or, what happened specifically?*
Involve others in the decision-making process and recognise their contribution: *When others have the chance to create the goals and game plan, they will be more accountable and committed to the results.*	*I'd like to you think about what teamwork is, why is matters, and how we can benchmark teamwork within our team. This alignment is an important precursor to creating our Team Charter. Let's cover each one of these now as a team.*

3

CONNECT INTO
OPPORTUNITY
THAT MATTERS

IMPROVE
YOURSELF AND
YOUR REULTS

CHAPTER 8

DARE TO
BE YOUR
BEST SELF

IMPROVE YOU AND IMPROVE YOUR GAME.

If you want to move confidently in the direction of your goals, invest your time and energy in your personal growth. Learn to work as hard on yourself as you do at your job—it will pay off.

Most people I work with don't have a grand career plan. In fact, most aren't clear on what their next role will be. But that doesn't stop them from wanting to learn and grow and take opportunities as they come along to move into bigger or different roles.

Are you giving your professional development the investment (time, energy, effort and money) you deserve? What if you focused your leadership through these lenses?

- results delivery (core, optimising core, innovating core depending on current results compared to performance benchmarks)
- developing others
- developing self.

Do you have a professional development plan? Is it a living/breathing document that you proactively use to plan and action your development goals? For most people I work with, the answer is no. They are heavily invested in implementation and results delivery because that is where their organisation's money is made, and through which their performance is measured. Achieving results is not getting easier. For many, we're working long hours, we're expected to do more with less, we're bombarded with emails (on average we get about 140 a day) and meeting requests, and there are too many demands on our time. We're under pressure and we are stressed. Consequently, these leaders don't have the time they would like to intentionally develop their team (to the degree they would like) or themselves.

IMPROVING RESULTS MEANS DEVELOPING OURSELVES.

Let's take this conversation back to you. For your personal and professional development needs to be met, it's essential that you have a clear awareness of what you want to achieve, what you need to get there, how you are progressing, what needs to change, and what will prevent you from getting there. That's why a coach can be a valuable resource to help you have the clarity and accountability you need.

A mentor once said to me, 'Your career will grow as fast as you're prepared to grow,' and I think that's valuable advice.

Nature teaches us that action creates clarity. Getting into action is a theme throughout this entire book. A pond with no running water will become murky so clarity in the water reduces. A pond, however, that features a running steam, will create clearness and clarity through movement. If you want more clarity, get into action, and you will find the clarity you seek.

Growth is hard, but you will not grow if you are not willing to change yourself.

So much of your game is not in your control. Top performers keep an eye on what they do control—themselves. Think of the people you know who do what it takes versus the people who are hoping, waiting and wishing for things to change. The people who achieve aren't smarter or more talented. They discern what is important, they take responsibility, and they are prepared to do the work. It's not rocket science. We have two key choices: we can let things happen or make things happen. Ultimately, you must take responsibility for your own development.

If you really want to do something you'll find a way. If you don't, you'll find an excuse.

—*Jim Rohn*

Living life as an enquiry makes learning and growing easier. Start where you are, then, one step at a time, improve the areas you choose. In her book Lean In, Sheryl Sandberg asks the question 'what would you do if you weren't afraid?'. In other words, if you knew you couldn't fail, what would you do? I think this is a great question to ask ourselves from time to time.

When using your leadership voice would you:

- be honest and tell your boss how you really feel?
- ask for help when you need it?
- speak up in forums and ask the question that's in your head?
- ask someone to explain something again or break it down for you in a way you understand?
- call people out on their bad behaviour or poor attitude?
- give someone the feedback they need to hear, including your boss?
- ask for commitments upfront rather than hoping people will do the right thing?
- not allow others to speak over you, ignore your contribution or dismiss it?
- put yourself forward for stretch opportunities to grow your skills and capabilities?
- go for the role even if there were parts of the role you couldn't do—yet?
- not worry so much about being judged?
- care less about being liked and care more about being effective?
- speak up for others in line with your personal standards?

WHAT WE CARE FOR CAN THRIVE.

Consider the areas in your life the you value the most, for example, your career, family relationships, personal relationships, financial security, health and wellbeing, and hobbies. Each requires time, energy and attention in order for you to feel satisfied with that particular area of your life. Everything we value and want to hold onto must be cared for, in order for it to thrive. This includes our growth and development within our career.

SMALL CHANGES OVER TIME WIN BIG RESULTS.

When you tap into your intrinsic motivation and take responsibility for creating the experiences you want (for example, feeling more confident, developing stronger relationships, initiating and driving a new project), you'll give yourself the greatest opportunity to make progress. In other words, the best way to step into your future is to link your effort to results through steps of progress.

Why is this so?

Professors Teresa Amabile and Stephen Krame pioneered The Progress Principle when they researched factors that influenced motivation at work. They found that making 'a clear sense of progress' was more influential on work motivation than goals, targets, incentives, rewards, or recognition of good work.

Goals, in themselves, aren't motivating. Setting goals and targets is easy; they represent the ideal of how we'd like things to be. However, the gap between intention and result is often what we don't want: the non-result. Goals can kickstart action but what motivates us along the way is a sense of progress.

BUSYNESS HINDERS THE RIGHT TYPE OF PROGRESS.

Any step is a step in the right direction, right? While I believe the answer is yes, I think the word 'right' is open to interpretation. What I'm acknowledging is the difference in the value of the steps. Therefore, the key question becomes how can we focus on making useful progress rather than progress that happens as a function of simply being busy and wanting to do 'stuff'? In addition, how can we remove the roadblocks getting in the way of useful progress?

The biggest roadblock we control is staying in our comfort zone. Staying in our comfort zone robs us of the chance to step into our potential.

Your next 10–20+% of incremental performance will come down to how well you can lead you outside your comfort zone. Leaning into your bigger game means creating the most empowered version of you. It means you leading you, and leading you means:

- taking responsibility for your personal and professional development

- seeking new challenges and opportunities to learn
- showing up ready to give it your best shot
- seeking constructive feedback to improve
- being a team player and enabling others to succeed also
- adapting to change and being prepared to do things differently
- thinking with the goal in mind and acting now
- focusing on the things that matter to drive your performance (discerning what is important and taking responsibility)
- getting into action now rather than waiting for the right time or the right something else
- appreciating that any result and non-result is simply feedback giving you an opportunity to learn something
- pushing through when things get tough
- bouncing back when things don't go your way
- being accountable for the commitments you make to yourself and others to deliver and achieve results.

WHAT IS YOUR POTENTIAL?

It's interesting to look at how you view your potential versus how others view it. Most people can't define potential for themselves in a way that is practically useful to them. Your potential is your ability to achieve with a level of capability you currently don't have yet. You realise your potential with every step forward in your growth and development. I believe that we have far more potential than we realise.

A question I often ask my clients is: are you better known for your results or your potential? This is a question you might not have thought about before and one you might struggle to answer because you can't see or measure it. The realisation many middle managers have is that they're known for their results. They've assumed their results will speak for themselves and they've stayed under the radar. The opportunity for them is to build their leadership voice and influence, so they become known for their potential (what they are capable of achieving in the future). You'll be much more likely to get a tap on the shoulder for a step up, when others can see your capacity for thinking, solving problems and leading change. You have to be visible for people to see what you can do. There's a point within middle management where results are expected; it's your brand—what you are known for—that matters more. I talk more about building a positive leadership brand in Chapter 10. On the flipside, the gaps between your present results and the results you could be achieving with your current level of capability is waste—your intellectual waste from you playing small.

CREATING CHANGE TAKES COURAGE
BUT KEEPING THINGS THE SAME
OFTEN CARRIES GREATER RISK.

No one likes change, really. It's easy to value what we have now because it's what we know, even though keeping things the same often carries greater risk. Spider monkeys are perfect examples of this. To catch spider monkeys, hunters in South America simply walk through the jungle and drop heavy containers on the ground. These containers have a narrow top and a wide bottom. The hunters drop nuts (a particular type the monkeys love) into the containers. Sometime later, the spider monkeys come down from the trees and smell the nuts. As the top of the container is so narrow, it's a tight squeeze to get their hands inside. Once they grab the nuts at the bottom and make a fist, they then can't get their hand out of the box while keeping hold of the nuts. So therein lies the problem: the monkey won't let go of the nuts (which it values) and doesn't have any idea that in not letting go of the nuts, it's giving up its freedom. So, instead of letting go of the nuts, the monkeys just sit there until the hunters come back, and pick them up.

I sometimes ask myself, what ideas, concepts or attachments do I need to be willing to give up in order to allow myself to grasp a bigger and better concept? Of what do I need to let go? I like to think of myself as a logical person, but I know I get attached to my ideas and my opinions; we all do. Sometimes it's hard to let go of what we know and what we perceive we value, but unless we do, we won't grow.

The most successful senior executives I've talked to share this commonality: the willingness to say yes to professional opportunities for themselves even when, for example, the timing isn't right, or they aren't sure they could do the role for which they were invited to apply. They say yes and figure out the 'how' later. To these executives, the risk of saying no, and waiting for another opportunity is far greater than the risk inherent in the opportunity to which they were saying yes.

CREATING OPPORTUNITY COMES DOWN TO
CREATING CHOICE, SEEING THE POSSIBILITY,
AND HAVING THE COURAGE AND PERSISTENCE
TO GET OUT OF YOUR COMFORT ZONE TO
SEE WHERE IT COULD LEAD.

Change starts with a conversation. How can you expand your networks and your thinking, challenge your assumptions, and create the space to think about what change you can put your name to?

High performers continuously seek new opportunities to demonstrate performance. Leaders who identify high-potential tactical/strategic opportunities and execute these opportunities with speed and confidence create a significant performance advantage. The bigger the challenge, the bigger the opportunity, and the more room for performance circle stretch. The bridge between being known as a deliverer and a leader is creating and driving new opportunity.

Saying yes to opportunity means:

Saying yes to not knowing the outcome.

Saying yes to failure.

Saying yes to learning.

Saying yes to doing this your entire life.

AIM FOR THE HIGHEST CLOUD.

The best sporting team of any sporting code in the world is the New Zealand All Blacks. They put their success down to team culture. At the core of their cultural philosophy is, 'better people make better All Blacks'. The All Blacks select on character over talent, which means some of New Zealand's most promising players never pull on the black jersey.

A culture of expectation enables the asking and re-asking of fundamental questions like: How can we do better? How do we keep moving forward, taking risks and taking personal responsibility?

Aim for the highest cloud is the All Black sentiment: create for yourself a narrative of extreme, even unrealistic ambitions, and benchmark yourself to the ultimate. Make it an epic narrative of what is possible.

WHAT DO YOU WANT?

What would 'nailing it' in your role look like over the next 12–24 months? What would you feel most proud of achieving? What would that mean for you? How would your development be reflected in that? How will you need to get out of your own way?

When you empower yourself with a daring and bold picture of success, believe that you can create it, and do what it takes, this is the formula for the journey ahead. The secret is to get out of your own way through the process, so you keep on going. Remember, change doesn't happen by chance, it happens by choice.

If you're going to play, you might as well play big.

—*Gail Kelly, Ex-CEO Westpac*

SHORT-TERM THINKING GETS IN THE WAY OF US BEING OUR BEST.

I asked Ben what he thought to be the overarching value of our coaching time together. He replied that he'd been able to discover things about himself that he hadn't realised before. This gave him a better appreciation of who he was and of what he was capable. I also asked him: What game do you want to play in the year ahead? What's going to be your best game? Ben went quiet. He realised he took a very short-term view of his role, which for him was completing the next milestone, and ticking off his current to-do list. He realised that his limited focus had impacted his growth. Being in the trees (the detail) wasn't giving him the picture of the forest (his big picture of success) that he wanted. He realised that playing big meant thinking big and then chunking it down into small manageable steps.

Some of the best questions a leader can ask themselves are:

1. How does my game need to change?
2. How do I need to change?
3. What do I need to start taking responsibility for?
4. What opportunity can I create?
5. If I'm not playing my best game, how will I get the position I want on the field?

Ultimately, have the courage to be you, not the version that you believe 'will look the best' in any given situation. Bring the version of you (all of you) who will serve others best. Bringing this version of you will empower you and others around you.

Are you ready to lean in and play bigger? Let's go.

CHAPTER 9

ACCELERATE YOUR LEARNING AND GROWTH

YOUR GROWTH STARTS
WITH YOUR PREPAREDNESS
AND WILLINGNESS TO LEARN.

Your bigger game is about being challenged and inspired to achieve next-level results. Big game players continuously develop their capabilities to learn, adapt and excel. Capability building is an active process. It requires continuous commitment as well as organisational support. Inherent in building capability is success and failure, both provide learning to reach the next level of mastery. Use these success principles to propel yourself forward.

1. MODEL SUCCESSFUL PEOPLE

Who do you admire and respect the most? Whose journey, experiences and results would you like to emulate?

When I first started my coaching journey, I attended an intensive training weekend led by Joe Pane, one of Australia's top coaches. Joe is a lead trainer at the Coaching Institute in Melbourne. The stories he shared brought his 8-year coaching journey to life in an inspiring way and watching him coach others was like nothing I'd ever experienced.

The act of him helping people created such profound shifts in their thinking. It lit me up, and I thought wow, maybe I could be just as amazing as that in eight years' time. So the next questions for me were what would I need to do in order to become a coach like that? Who would I need to become?

Modelling is about achieving an outcome by studying how someone else goes about it; it's more than learning the actions and behaviours.

I was once talking with a mentor who was on track to make $800K in her coaching and training practice that year. Over coffee, we talked about the things she'd done in order to reach this financial milestone. As we were talking, I was aware that I was focusing on 'what she did' to reach this success. In reflection, my focus was well intended but I fell into the same trap others do. One of the easiest mistakes is to model someone by only focusing on what they've done to achieve success, believing that replicating the same actions will achieve the same or similar success. This thinking is flawed.

Effective modelling involves building a four-dimensional view of someone. Knowing what she did is only a piece of the puzzle. It's the starting point. We need to move beyond that to see a four-dimensional perspective of them. We need to see this picture before we can begin to model.

Modelling someone to see the full picture involves four elements:

1a. Study their thinking about:
- values and beliefs
- goals and purpose (the 'why' of what their success will give them)
- standards (where do they hold the line on 'what', no matter what)
- rituals (the habits they develop to structure time and energy in doing the things they do)
- attitudes (on what they do, and life in general).

1b. Study how they structure their actions:
- What do they focus on (which will be a function of the results they get)?
- How do they make decisions?
- What do they consider and evaluate choice?
- What benchmarks do they have to check their progress to determine if they are on track?

1c. Study what they do:
- What actions do they take?
- What sequence do they follow to focus their actions?
- How do they measure actions and results?

- What is their criterion to know how to adjust actions and what to adjust when required?

1d. Study who they involve:
- Who do they have on their 'A' team?
- What do they expect of others who are supporting them?
- What company do they keep?

Modelling is so much more than knowing and doing what they do. It involves understanding the perspective(s) they have, how their thinking is shaped, and the relationship they have with themselves. Creating success is based on all four of the above dimensions, which must be functioning effectively to shape the results we can achieve. Asking quality questions is the best way to build a 4-dimensional picture of the person you want to model.

In summary, knowing the actions someone took, without understanding the thinking behind the actions, is not that useful. Here's an example: creating success often means building great relationships. When we model effectively, we find out the difference that made the difference. The fact that they strived to be interested more than be interesting, that they put someone else's needs ahead of their own, that they were obsessed about making them feel valued, and they took the time to understand how they could be valuable.

If creating success was just about a list of tasks, then we'd all be successful. By understanding this 'full picture', we see what's actually needed to succeed—this is how to model someone effectively.

Remember to explore connections and relationships in and out of work that offer role-modelling opportunities. For example, community groups, sports, or your extended professional/ personal network may have leaders worth reaching out to.

NEVER STOP LEARNING.

Learning supports a continuous cycle of growth and development. The model below shows the keys to learning how others can champion and support you, and how you can champion yourself.

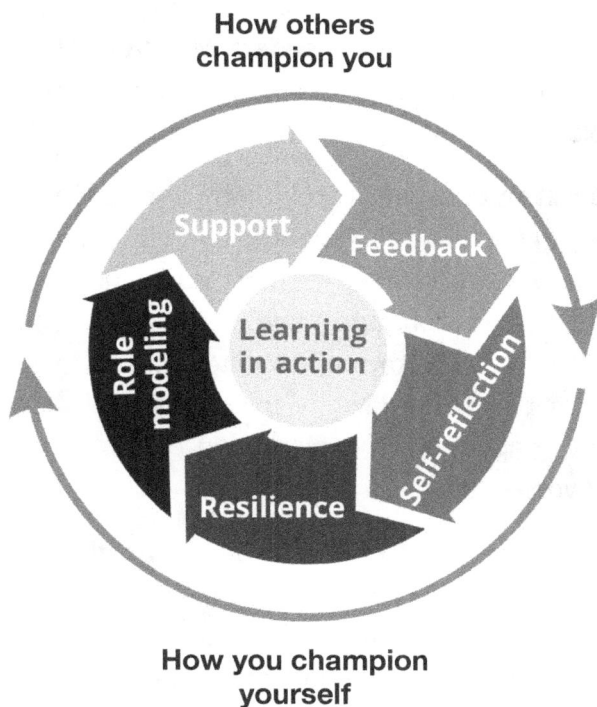

**How others
champion you**

Support

Feedback

Learning
in action

Role
modeling

Self-reflection

Resilience

**How you champion
yourself**

FIGURE 9: CONTINUOUS CYCLE OF LEARNING MODEL

2. GET THE SUPPORT YOU NEED

In theory, a great way to learn is through effective coaching and mentoring from your boss, but unfortunately, the reality for many leaders is quite different. I work with clients who perceive they don't have inspiring direct role models to learn leadership from, nor do they have formal/informal mentoring in place. Often, they perceive their ideal mentor as too high up, too busy, or they fear being rejected if a mentoring request is turned down.

The most successful leaders have had mentors (often, more than one at a time) through their leadership journey. They've been proactive in identifying leaders who can champion their development in the short term and become sponsors for future role opportunities.

Years ago, in my corporate career, I was displaced from a Head of Marketing role due to a new Managing Director coming on board who brought her own Head of Marketing. The new MD had a great reputation, and I had a choice: to focus on the unfairness of it all with my pride shattered, or to focus on how I could turn it into a positive by, for example, plucking up the courage to capitalise on a mentoring opportunity with her. She said yes—thankfully.

When I look back on my corporate career and the people who have helped guide me, I can't help but wonder what could have been if I had invested more in those relationships and done a better job of extracting more value from them.

You must consider mentoring relationships (informal or formal) over the long term as well as the short term. For example, you might have 6–8 people who are significant in your life, who you can learn from, whose perspectives you value, who challenge you, who believe in you. Choose people from different facets of your life whose perspective you value and whose thinking is different to your own. The quality of your life is a reflection of your environment and the quality of relationships you have. Who is championing your professional development and career? Are you listening to advice and seeking advice from people whose advice is worth listening to?

> **You're the average of the five people you spend most of your time with.**
>
> *—Jim Rohn*

Your mentor will want to help you, but you need to establish what help you need from them and why you need it. You must demonstrate your commitment to creating the positive change you seek.

Here's some tips on how to capitalise on short term mentoring arrangements:

1. Be clear on the areas you want to develop and why they are a priority
2. Seek out people who are strong in the areas you want to develop. Don't be afraid to find mentors who are different than you in terms of personality and style. It forces you to think about yourself. A mentor who will validate your thinking will give you confidence, but they

won't help you move forward. There is a lot to value in diversity that can help shape your thinking.

3. Set up short-term mentoring arrangements with a specific objective(s), a finite number of mentoring sessions (weekly, fortnightly or monthly). Align on what success looks like and base your conversations on progress being made and next steps of progress. Be prepared for the session with your mentor, and if possible, make the relationship a value exchange. Look for how you might be able to give value back to your mentor. This may not be obvious at first, but don't be put off by that.

Remember that developing relationships with mentors is a strategic opportunity to position you and your potential. By having a larger number of short-term mentoring relationships (and some relationships might continue), you'll build a network of sponsors who can support and champion your career advancement. Never underestimate the value in having more senior leaders in your corner—you may need them when you least expect it.

3. SEEK FEEDBACK AS A GIFT

Leadership is perception. Perception is powerful. We form perceptions of others based on our first impressions, observations, past and current experiences, values and beliefs, and biases. In Chapter 1, I explained how we all have a unique map for how we experience the world. This is why feedback is simply someone else's perception; it's not the truth but it's their truth.

We get feedback throughout our day. Every interaction results in a response; it's all feedback. It's our choice to see it as a gift rather than something to judge or defend in a way that makes us right or look better/worse. Overlaying judgement gets in the way of being able to see ourselves accurately. How we judge feedback gets in our way of learning from it.

Receiving feedback is a valuable way for someone to know and understand the perceptions of others have of them and what's driving those perceptions. With this insight, managers and leaders can better understand how they can become more self-aware and effective.

Feedback is about continuous learning; it's an attitude. You have to be willing to listen to feedback; it's a daily exercise. It's not a certain time. Receiving feedback takes courage. Be brave. If you ask, you need to be prepared to listen and take it on. When you do, people will give you more.
—*Alice Wong*

People are naturally curious about themselves, which is why personality, behavioural, and team profiling tools can be such fascinating experiences. Obtaining 360-degree feedback will give you diverse perspectives from your boss, peers/colleagues and your direct team so you can compare the perceptions across your spheres of influence.

Although we like getting good feedback, we don't like getting critical feedback that leaves us feeling like we've failed or we're not good enough. I believe most people are starved of useful feedback.

People want to be empowered. They want effective feedback to develop skills and build confidence that will help them succeed. The benefits of gathering specific, meaningful and ongoing feedback outweigh the challenges. It goes beyond measuring how well you met the goals or deadlines. It uncovers how your colleagues feel about working with you, how you communicate and collaborate with them, and how you handle stress, change and adversity. Without feedback, people tend to be self-congratulatory or overly self-critical.

ARE YOU BEING PROACTIVE AND SEEKING OUT FEEDBACK THAT WILL AID YOU BECOME MORE EFFECTIVE?

My clients often tell me they're not getting feedback, and if they are it's not insightful, helpful or timely. In encouraging responsibility, I like to challenge their thinking by asking 'Why have you made your boss responsible for giving you feedback? Instead, I encourage my clients to come up with a specific development objective, share it with their boss and specify the type of feedback they'd like, then book an informal catch up in 1–3 months' time. This approach creates a window of opportunity for their boss to tune into something on which to observe them. If your boss is tuned in to the feedback you want, chances are, they will be much better at providing useful feedback on demand.

4. INVEST IN QUALITY SELF-REFLECTION

Self-reflection builds self-awareness: who we are being for ourselves, who we are being for others and how we are creating the experience someone else has of us.

Quality self-reflection is an attitude—you can't teach this. It starts with the daily practice of seeing yourself in a way that evaluates why you are doing things: you are looking at yourself from the eyes of someone else. It's about seeing different perspectives and choosing the perspective that will serve others.

—Carlos Schafer

Leadership is a journey of self-learning and self-improvement. Your leadership effectiveness relies on your ability to think reflectively, to see in perspective and in context where there is only interpretation. Being self-effective is a continual process of self-reflection to see and evaluate yourself through different lenses and perspectives, giving you insight that will enable you to improve your critical thinking, decision making, influence, impact, and results. Most importantly though, we can be at cause rather than at effect—this is an empowering choice.

Continual self-reflection is a way that helps you see yourself and gauge how others might perceive you. The purpose is not to judge you, rather to look at what you learned and what you can apply next time, in a way that acknowledges the effort you've made to take you closer to the result you want.

Often people don't want to do their own self-diagnosis, and they then wonder why they are not able to impact, influence and inspire their team and colleagues. Engaging in quality self-reflection should be a daily habit, one that lifts you up rather than criticises and pulls you down.

Here is my Four R's Reflective Model to outline the key steps involved in self-reflection:

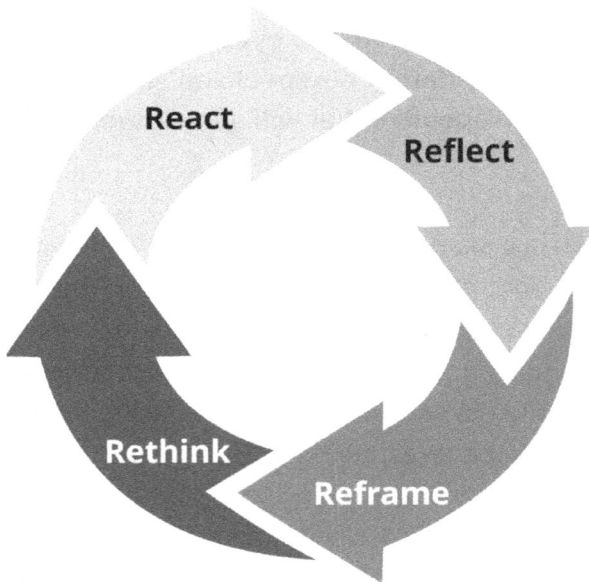

FIGURE10: FOUR 'R'S REFLECTIVE MODEL

Reflect: Differentiate between the event (what happened) and what meaning you gave to the event (what you made it mean). Nothing has meaning except for the meaning you give it.

For example: I've been told one of my direct reports complained about my micro-management style (this is what happened). I need to find out which one of my direct reports obviously doesn't like me anyone (this is what I made it mean).

Reframe: This involves looking at the event through different lenses to enable you to appreciate different perspectives. All meaning is context dependant. In any situation, there are many more meanings and interpretations than the ones we can see. In other words, reframing means creating a different way of looking at a situation, person, or relationship in order to think or feel differently about it.

For example: I'm grateful to know how I'm viewed by this person. I'd rather know than not know how he/she feels about my leadership so I can improve things.

Resilient people are very good at reframing, for example, to reframe something that could be seen as challenging to something that is motivating and positive.

Rethink: Choose a perspective that will serve you resourcefully.

For example: Getting this feedback provides an opportunity for me to seek additional feedback that will help me ascertain how I could be more effective for my team.

React: Take action

For example: I'll meet with this direct report today, and create the space for us to align on how we can work together and meet both our needs.

5. BUILD YOUR RESILIENCE BECAUSE THINGS WON'T ALWAYS GO YOUR WAY

If leadership is a journey of self-discovery and growth, then your resilience are the pages on which your story is written.

Sometimes things don't work out the way we want: we lose our jobs, our role changes, we work for bosses we don't like, we work with people we'd prefer not to, our projects get reprioritised, the budget gets cut or the goal posts change. People undermine us or don't support us when we need them. Sometimes we get surprised, we get a jolt, we get hurt, we get angry and we get knocked down. This is the journey of life, right? You never know what is around the corner.

However, when you're down, the only direction is up. The more adversity you've faced and overcome the more resilient you'll be. The more resilience you have, the more risk and uncertainty you can manage and overcome.

Resilience is your ability to recover from setbacks and adapt to change; it's a mental strength that allows you to keep going in the face of adversity. Resilience is how you lead you when things are tough. Resilient people don't wallow or dwell on failures; they acknowledge the situation, learn from their mistakes, and move forward. Being challenged—sometimes severely—is part of what activates resilience as a skill set. Resilience is the ability of leaders to manage their own personal responses and reactions in a fast-paced environment.

The biggest driver of your performance is your emotional intelligence. Resilience is a key factor in your capacity to manage your emotions and your mindset.

No one can teach you how to do resilience. I can't teach you how to be resilient (resilience is more than a model, process or a framework). Rather, it's a capacity you have that is developed through your experiences. It's something you tap into and turn on when you need it. It's a muscle, and I want to show you some distinctions/dimensions of resilience, so you can develop a resilience mindset and build your resilience muscle.

WE ARE MORE RESILIENT THAN WE REALISE.

Resilience means different things to different people. For some, it's relevant only when big things go wrong, for others, it's something that helps them get through their day.

To me, resilience is all about keeping calm and carrying on. I single-parent two young children. I have no direct family support here, and I'm still in the first seven years of building my business. I juggle many different balls at once and try to keep it all together. Some days, are easier than others. When I tap into my resilience, I shape a conversation with myself where I acknowledge that:

- It's okay to feel that things are not okay.
- It's okay to feel how I feel (whether that's sad, frustrated or angry).

- It's okay to stuff up; I'm not perfect.
- Regardless of how I feel and what is going on, I'm okay … everything is okay. I'm still enough, and I have everything I need within me to move forward
- Things are going to get better. What can I learn from where I'm at with this?

Ultimately, I'm responsible for everything that happens in my life. I choose to believe I'm the driver of every choice I make.

ORGANISATIONS ARE ONLY AS RESILIENT AS THE PEOPLE WITHIN THEM.

Resilience is regarded as one of the most critical leadership competencies. A new Australian workplace survey has revealed 73% of workers are stressed about work and stressed workers are 2½ times more likely to look for a new job in the next year than those who are not stressed.[xviii]

The biggest stressors in our workplace include pressure to deliver against volume of workload and pace, poor leadership, conflict, relationships, politics, communication, and how things get done. Given the predictions around the nature of work, accelerating pace of change, and ongoing complexity and ambiguity in our working environments, resilience is a necessary leadership trait.

Resilience comprises the following four pillars:

BELIEF	ATTITUDE	DECISION	ACTION
Trust in the process that will enable you to achieve a goal and/or for something to get better	Willingness to take responsibility	Commitment to a way forward and taking the next step	Persistence: doing what it takes to get there

Your ability to do all of this relies on you:

a) **accepting** the reality as it is
b) **choosing** a perspective that will serve you best
c) **adapting** to have the sensory acuity to change what you do and how you do it in as many ways as it takes to achieve the result you want.

Do you have the resilience you need to overcome your challenges? What could you accomplish if you had the strength not to give up?

BE OPTIMISTIC.

As Brian Tracy says, 'Optimism is the one quality more associated with success and happiness than any other'.

Having resilience means maintaining enthusiasm on the days when you're sailing through and the inevitable days when you feel out of your depth.

It's easy to be excited when it's all new and shiny. It's easy when it's more of the same. If you can't keep up your enthusiasm, you're going to play small, play safe or quit along the way and not pass through to the next level. You're not going to know what it's like on the other side. It's worth it to find out.

—*Sharon Pearson*

Being optimistic means interpreting setbacks, challenges, and failure as something temporary and changeable. For example, it's not going away quickly but it's just this one situation, and I can do something about it. It's not just about positive thinking but realising that when things go wrong, the painful situation holds an opportunity to learn and grow. Oftentimes, the greater the hurt, the greater the lesson.

DON'T BE ATTACHED TO THE OUTCOME.

Being attached to an outcome is a recipe for disappointment. Things don't always go according to plan. Things can change along the way. Being committed to a goal is one thing and being fixed on one path to get there is another. It's much better to stay open, flexible and relaxed about outcomes and how you reach them.

Resilient people never think of themselves as victims. Instead, they focus their time and energy on changing the things over which they have control. They are able to let go of everything else and take responsibility for their actions. As a result, they are much more able to think quickly and creatively, and discover a new path or an alternative solution.

DON'T SWEAT THE SMALL STUFF.

Working life is full of every day challenges: big ones, small ones, some we expect and some we don't.

Be aware of how much you react to what happens in your day. The degree to which we create emotion, drama and stress is relative to the severity of the situation and shows our capability to see things with a resourceful perspective.

When we experience stress, even if it's just a moment of exasperation, the cortisol levels in our bodies change. These small surges of hormone can add up and have a detrimental effect on our wellbeing. Not only that, when we let little things get to us, we are far more likely to drown in stress and negativity when larger challenges present themselves. So let go of the little things; don't react to them. There are bigger things that are worth your time, energy and effort.

BE KIND AND COMPASSIONATE.

We all perceive that we fail from time to time. It's life.

It's important to be kind to yourself, give yourself a break, and see the bigger picture at play. After all, your career isn't a straight line. Your success is not guaranteed. You can be doing all the right things and things will still go wrong. Setbacks and stuff-ups are built into the rollercoaster ride of working life for a reason: to enable you to push past what you thought was possible; to help you learn something about yourself; to help you respond better next time; and to create new possibility. Your success is doing that for your entire career.

Resilient people are empathetic and compassionate. They maintain healthy relationships, and reach out for help and support when they need it. However, they don't waste time worrying what others think of them, and they don't bow to peer pressure.

LOOK AFTER YOURSELF.

We're often so busy looking after everyone and everything else, that we don't take as good of care of ourselves as we need. Resilience is not only mental, it's also physical.

That's why it's important to nourish our bodies and create the balance we need to tackle challenges. Figure out what balance means for you. Eating well, exercising regularly and getting enough sleep are great ways to keep well. Making sure you take regular breaks at work and creating clear work-life boundaries also helps.

HAVE FUN. BE PLAYFUL.

When I ask executives what advice they would give their younger selves, there is a consistent answer: Don't take things too seriously, it's not 'that' serious. Take things lightly and enjoy the ride. The ride is your life, it's not the destination.

CHAPTER 10

BUILD YOUR BRAND CONSCIOUSLY

HAVING A GOOD LEADERSHIP BRAND STARTS WITH SELF-BELIEF.

If there is one fundamental leadership truth, it is this: our self-belief is the basis of what we see is possible for ourselves — what we can achieve. If you remember, we started this journey together by venturing inward, to the core of who you are, to your self-identity.

Through greater influence, we can all make a significant positive difference to others and in the process, learn and grow into the next best versions of ourselves. This is the journey of leadership development and the journey we've been through this book. In other words, when we improve ourselves, we can contribute more of ourselves to others. We have more to give. It's an inside-out process. We move from what we know and **believe about ourselves** (our self-beliefs) to **what others believe about us** and our potential (our leadership identity or brand). For this reason, I want to finish this book talking specifically about brand. Your leadership brand reflects the influence you have. The greater your spheres of influence, the better your leadership brand will be.

YOU ARE KNOWN FOR YOUR LEADERSHIP BRAND.

Whether we're aware of it, we all have a brand. How often do you reflect on yours? Your actions, decisions, and attitude drive how others perceive you. Your brand is your perceived business worth (your value proposition). Your brand isn't static; it is created in every interaction through which others experience you and your leadership.

Your brand is a function of how you show up, the quality of relationships you have, and your ability to drive and deliver results and effective change. These three key elements have been addressed throughout this book and are the focus for this chapter. Depending on your specific development needs, building your brand means lifting your performance in one or more of these areas. Why? Because your growth in these areas will positively change the perceptions others have of you. When you play bigger, your brand will improve.

STEP INTO YOUR POTENTIAL AND SPARK YOUR BIGGER GAME.

McKinsey Research has consistently shown that one of the key non-financial motivators for high performance is 'creating opportunities' for career/professional/performance growth.

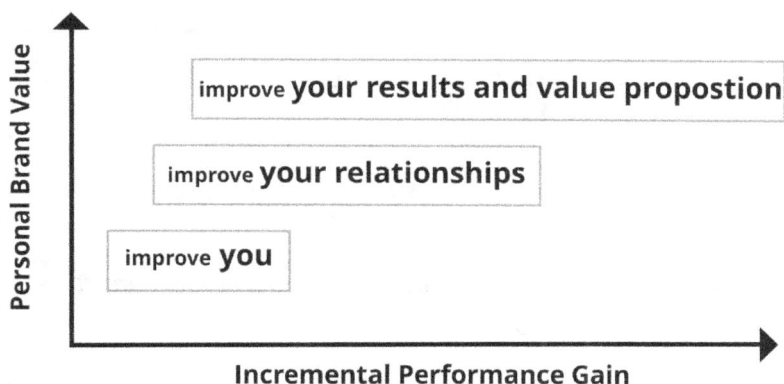

FIGURE 12: WHERE IS YOUR INCREMENTAL PERFORMANCE LIFT?

Building influence happens in the context of your overall performance. Ask yourself: where will my next 10–30% level of incremental performance come from? I'm trusting that while you were reading this book, you had some 'a-ha' moments that sparked some insight for your leadership journey ahead. Do you have the clarity and direction you need to step into your bigger game? There is more to influence than meets the eye isn't there? Let me provide a useful and simple framework for your 'where to from here?' thinking, in a way that brings the chapters of this book together.

Your bigger game lies within three interconnected areas of opportunity:

- Improve you **(connect into you).**
- Improve your relationships **(connect into others).**
- Improve your results **(connect into opportunity that matters).**

All three parts of your game need to be working effectively for you to build influence and grow your leadership brand.

IMPROVE YOU:

Building influence has to start with you: who you are for you and a commitment to improving you.

It's believed that 90% of leadership is self-leadership. Leading others starts with leading you. This means, for example, developing a functional mindset, being true to your values and principles, and leveraging your strengths. Find out what makes you tick, and accept and value who you are, and that of which you are capable. Become more self-certain, as it's the key to building greater confidence.

Ask yourself, if you were true to your values and principles, how would you show up as a leader every day? Whether you manage others doesn't matter, it's about being consistent with who you are and how you want others to perceive you. This is how to lead intentionally and authentically.

Improving you also includes your productivity. Focus on the things that matter the most to drive your performance. The people who achieve aren't smarter or more talented, they discern what is important, take responsibility, and focus what matter. It's that black and white. Don't wait and wish for things to change—decide and get into action. Confidence, courage, and resilience all happen when you're in action.

IMPROVE YOUR RELATIONSHIPS:

Being the best at anything doesn't matter unless you can work with and through others to achieve results. Your results are a direct reflection of the quality of your relationships.

Your network, connections and relationships are the funnels for you to share, learn and grow. Expanding your knowledge and capacity for thinking is critical to your leadership growth. At your core, you're social and emotional. Whether you're extroverted or introverted, learning how to work with different personalities and group dynamics is essential. Trust is the foundation of any relationship, starting with you being trustworthy. Proactively invest into your relationships and find ways to build credibility and your leadership voice through the process.

IMPROVE YOUR RESULTS:

Solid performers and high performers are separated by opportunities they pursue not by talent or potential. Build influence through achieving results that matter.

To determine where the biggest opportunities are in your role (being mindful of your business situation and delivering to the strategic agenda), think of the 'core' of your role/operation as the engine that drives 80%+ of your results. Then consider your engine and determine whether your focus should be to:

a) Rev it up: **focus on core** (focus here if your KPI's are not being met).
b) Turbo fuel it: **optimise core** (focus here if your KPI's are being met consistently).
c) Build the next engine (focus here if you're ready to transform your results)—**innovate core.**

Deciding on whether your focus needs to be within core, optimising core, or innovating core is a great place to start. For example, focusing on having the latest range of cool magazines for waiting customers will be redundant if the average customer waiting time means you're losing customers.

Your next level results rely on you stepping into spaces, and driving and owning change that matters, rather than simply contributing to it. It's about stepping into spaces where you create and deliver, rather than just being a part of the team. Seizing opportunity requires courage—the courage to step outside your comfort zone and out of your own way, and into your growth and development.

**If somebody offers you an amazing opportunity
but you are not sure you can do it, say yes,
then learn how to do it later.**

—Richard Branson

You need to create personal accountability to show you can wrap your around something that delivers results. You have to be able to look back and answer the following questions about your performance:

1. What did I deliver?
2. What positive change did I lead?
3. What did I cause?

Leaders who identify high-potential tactical/strategic opportunities and execute these opportunities with speed and confidence create a significant performance advantage. The bigger the challenge, the bigger the opportunity and the more room for performance circle stretch.

Any change starts with a conversation: how can you expand your networks, expand your thinking, challenge your assumptions, and create the space to think about what change you can put your name to?

Within these three areas of opportunity—improve you, improve your relationships, and improve your results— where are your greatest opportunities to shine? What is your inner voice telling you?

YOU ARE READY.

You have what it takes. It's time to step into your worth and value. It's time to see you for who you really are and for who you can be. You deserve to give that back to you. It's also time for others to see the potential you have. You've got this. I'm excited for you and what's possible for you. I trust you're feeling excited too.

YOUR DEVELOPMENT AND HOW TO ACCOMPLISH IT

SET OR RESET YOUR LEADERSHIP DEVELOPMENT GOALS.

Many people don't have any development goals, they have too many of them, or they have loose annual goals that can be put off until the time is right. Deciding to focus on a few development goals at once can help you dedicate the time, energy and effort where you can make the most beneficial progress. Your goals can start with what makes the most sense to you, but remember to chunk them down into milestones and steps so you can track your progress.

It's better to achieve a few big things really well than a lot of things not very well.

Be clear on where your development focus needs to be. If you had the level of influence you desire, what would be different? How would you be different? How would others interact and respond to you differently? How will that change be reflected in your leadership? How does your leadership need to change?

Below is a simple template (if you'd like one) to map out your development focus, goals, and actions toward building your leadership influence. I encourage you to choose three key areas of development focus over the next 90 days. Why?.

- You can create some urgency (vs a 12-month development goal) in a good way. It gives you time to put your goals into action and see some tangible results to track your progress.
- Up to three development areas every 90 days will give you (up to) 12 areas of focus over the year. Three development goals at once is the maximum I would recommend. Top performers give their development the dedicated focus and attention it deserves. Think about what this focus would mean for you over the next 12 months.
- The timeframe can work well with your boss as a check-in for where you're at, where you're headed, and what support you need from your boss. If he/she is aware of your development goals then this timeframe works well in terms of getting feedback within a period where you can make observable progress.

The biggest challenge in rolling 90-day development plans is being 100% accountable and responsible for you and your development. As with anything, great intentions don't achieve great results but committing and doing what it takes to consistently achieve does.

You might know what these are already but if not, here are some ideas to get you started.

- Developing self-awareness
- Develop emotional EQ—align intention with impact
- Building self-certainty: developing inner confidence, trust and esteem
- Personal effectiveness: enhancing the ability to focus, discern priorities, say 'no' and let go
- Developing leadership identity, presence and voice
- Develop leadership benchmarks to lead from the front, side and behind
- Developing behavioural flexibility: adapting leadership style to engage and influence across diverse groups and personalities
- Be able to present confidently in any forum
- Building a communication toolkit that can engage and influence others
- Having tough conversations the right way
- Giving empowering feedback
- Leading effective change
- Developing and communicating a vision
- Being decisive and making effective decisions
- Dealing with stress and pressure

- Building a coaching toolkit to empower others
- Managing up/leading up
- Leadership effectiveness: building the foundations and benchmarks for a high performing team.

I've completed a worksheet to provide an example of how to breakdown goals, milestones and actions. Your ability to think sequentially, that is, breakdown goals into specific tasks, is important for your development. Having a great goal is one thing, but it must translate into the specific actions that will enable you to achieve it.

So, this is it. You're on your own. I've loved taking you on this journey. Thank you for your curiosity, thank you for leaning in, and thank you for believing in you enough to step into the opportunity in front of you. Now you need to do the work. Now you need to show what you've got within you. Remember, you've got this. You always have.

I look forward to hearing about your success.

BUILDING INFLUENCE WORKSHEET - LEADERSHIP DEVELOPMENT AREA ONE

What I want to achieve: Proactively build trust with a few of my direct team

MILESTONE	ACTIONS
Demonstrate more respect	1) Become more conscious of the feelings and sensitivities in my team. 2) Be less judgmental and proactively seek different perspectives.
Have open and honest conversations	1) Acknowledge someone in the team per day for their effort/behaviour. 2) Send out an update to the team that reflects progress in the month against target (to rally the team).
Align on shared purpose/goals	1) In 1:1 conversations ask the report about future aspirations are and have a meaningful short conversation that aligns to their development goals. 2) Book in next team offsite and review the existing team charter. Do we need to update?
Develop greater confidence in each others' abilities	1) When delegating, be clear on the goal of the task/initiative, align on the steps required and who is responsible for the follow-up or check-in. 2) Create a stretch opportunity for someone in the team and brief them/engage them on it.

Benchmarks for progress (how I know I'm succeeding):

I will have deeper, more open and honest conversations, better communication and have more influence with my team. I'll feel a greater sense of 'my team are with me' – I've got their back and they've got mine. This will come from a place of really knowing, rather than from a place of hoping that everything's okay on a transactional day-to-day level.

LEADERSHIP DEVELOPMENT AREA ONE:

What I want to achieve:

MILESTONE	ACTIONS

Benchmarks for progress (how I know I'm succeeding):

LEADERSHIP DEVELOPMENT AREA **TWO**:

What I want to achieve:

MILESTONE	ACTIONS

Benchmarks for progress (how I know I'm succeeding):

LEADERSHIP DEVELOPMENT AREA **THREE**:

What I want to achieve:

MILESTONE	ACTIONS

Benchmarks for progress (how I know I'm succeeding):

ABOUT THE AUTHOR

Toni drives the results, team development and profitability of every organisation with which she works. Her mission is to empower leaders and teams to lean in and spark a bigger game.

Transition has been a central theme in both Toni's personal and professional life. She has led teams through significant organisational change and has held a range of roles within emerging and mature businesses. She is known for her drive, resilience, and high energy.

Toni is engaged to instigate growth and improve performance. Her conviction is that people are capable of much more than they think—her practice is to help them achieve it.

Toni empowers leaders and teams to fast track their leadership and performance, and prepares leaders for starting new roles, accelerating within current roles, or getting role ready for a step-up position.

With an extensive blue chip commercial background Toni brings over 20 years' experience in building and leading high-performance teams. She has served in senior leadership roles in New Zealand, the UK, the USA and Australia working for brands including ANZ, Westpac, American Express and Deloitte.

Toni is a certified Executive Coach and Trainer, and a Practitioner in Neuro-Linguistic Programming. She holds a Bachelor of Business Management (First Class Hons). She runs her practice as a coach/mentor, trainer, facilitator and speaker.

WORKING WITH TONI

Thank you for reading *Influence from the inside out*. I'm trusting it's given you the insight, direction, and inspiration you need to spark your bigger game.

While there is no silver bullet to your personal or professional development, the right strategies and support will accelerate your growth.

Some of the most worthwhile questions a leader can ask are:

'Toni, it feels like you are sitting on my shoulder'.

- How does my game need to change?
- What is the next best version of me (in this new game)?
- If I'm not playing my A-Game, how will I have the position on the field (that is, the level of influence) I want?

If you (or your team) are serious about finding the solutions to these questions, playing your bigger game and receiving additional support, don't hesitate to reach out. Although I'm based in Melbourne, I travel internationally to help organisations align their leadership teams to where they need to be.

In the meantime, I'd like to invite you to receive my regular bursts of leadership thinking. You can subscribe free at www. tonicourtney.com. On my website, you will also find further free downloadable resources.

So how can I begin to help you? It all starts with a conversation, right? I'd love to hear about your progress. Please contact me at www.tonicourtney.com or toni@tonicourtney.com with details of your successes and failures along the way—after all, it's all part of the journey.

Cheers

WORKS CITED

Amabile, T. & Krame, S., 2011. The progress principle. *Harvard Business Review Press.*

Brown, B., 2010. *The gifts of imperfection: let go of who you think you're supposed to be and embrace who you are.* s.l.:Hazelden Publishing.

Chamorro-Premuzic, T., Wade, M. & Jordan, J., 2018. As AI makes more decisions, the nature of leadership will change. *Harvard Business Review*, 22 January.

Dweck, C., 2007. *Mindset: The new psychology of success.* s.l.:Ballantine Books.

Eurich, T., 2018. What self-awwareness really is (and how to cultivate it). *Havard Business Review,* 4 January.

Harris, D. R., 2010. *The confidence gap: From fear to freedom.* s.l.:Penguin Books Australia.

Holiday, R. & Hanselman, S., 2016. *The daily stoic: 366 medications on wisdom, perserverance, and the art of living.* s.l.:Penguin Publishing Group.

Malley, A., 2014. *The naked CEO: The truth you need to build a big life.* s.l.:Wiley.

Maxwell, J., 2011. *The 360 Ddegree Leader: Developing your influence from anywhere in the organization. Reprint ed.* s.l.:HarperCollins Leadership.

Robbins, A., 1992. *Awaken the giant within: How to take immediate control of your mental, emotional, physical and financial destiny.* s.l.:Free Press.

Taleb, N. N., 2014. *Antifragile: Things that gain from disorder. Reprint ed.* s.l.:Random House Trade Paperbacks.

TEDxBloomington, 2011. *Shawn Achor: The happy secret to better work.* [Online] Available at: https://www.ted.com/talks/shawn_achor_the_happy_secret_to_better_work

WEBSITES CITED

www.gallup.com/services/190118/engaged-workplace.aspx

www.swinburneleadershipinstitute.wordpress.com

www.hbr.org

ENDNOTES (WEBSITE REFERENCE LINKS)

[i] https://www.christianitytoday.com/pastors/2007/july-online-only/090905.html

[ii] http://newsroom.melbourne.edu/news/survey-australian-business-reveals-failure-leadership

[iii] https://www.theceomagazine.com/business/management-leadership/investing-in-leadership-development-skillset-or-mindset/

[iv] https://developingchild.harvard.edu/resources/three-core-concepts-in-early-development/

[v] www.earlychildhoodaustralia.org.au¬

[vi] https://www.forbes.com/sites/kathycaprino/2018/02/03/transformational-leaders-the-top-trait-that-separates-them-from-the-rest/3/#da0e7e41a98d

[vii] https://www.forbes.com/sites/joannafurlong/2018/01/13/pbs-ceo-paula-kerger-on-how-she-got-to-ceo-and-why-leadership-is-not-for-everyone/2/#93654de14c70

[viii] https://www.smh.com.au/lifestyle/health-and-wellness/most-women-hate-their-body-heres-how-to-stop-20160129-gmgweo.html

[ix] https://hbr.org/2018/01/what-self-awareness-really-is-and-how-to-cultivate-it

[x] https://hbr.org/2018/01/podcast-women-at-work

[xi] https://hbr.org/2018/01/perfectionism-is-increasing-and-thats-not-good-news

[xii] https://www.forbes.com/sites/michaelsimmons/2015/01/15/this-is-the-1-predictor-of-career-success-according-to-network-science/#581ff383e829

[xiii] https://www.weforum.org/reports/the-future-of-jobs-report-2018

[xiv] https://www.acs.org.au/content/dam/acsacs-documents/16-0026_DATA61_REPORT_TomorrowsDigiallyEnabledWorkforce_WEB_160128.pdf

[xv] https://www.forbes.com/sites/travisbradberry/2014/01/09/emotional-intelligence/#7ee45d091ac0

[xvi] http://www.kornferry.com/developing-learning-agility

[xvii] https://hbr.org/2016/11/why-diverse-teams-are-smarter

[xviii] https://www.theaustralian.com.au/life/workplace-stress-affects-73-per-cent-of-employees/news-story/2495662b85e6ef95ee5792f11b9c46ea